D0901189

Rome in the Bible and the Early Church

Rome in the Bible and the Early Church

Edited by Peter Oakes

PATERNOSTER PRESS

A Division of Baker Book House Co

BUFFALO GROVE PUBLIC LIBRARY
100 EAST SOUH STREET
CHICAGO, ILLINOIS 60615

BS
2545
.R65
R66
2002

Copyright © 2002 Peter Oakes and the Contributors
First published in 2002 by Paternoster Press

08 07 06 05 04 03 02   7 6 5 4 3 2 1

Paternoster Press is an imprint of Authentic Media,
P.O. Box 300, Carlisle, Cumbria, CA3 0QS, UK
Website: www.paternoster-publishing.com

Baker Academic is a division of Baker Book House Company
P.O. Box 6287, Grand Rapids, MI 49516-6287
Website: www.bakeracademic.com

The right of Peter Oakes and the Contributors to be identified as the Authors
of this Work has been asserted by them in accordance with the Copyright,
Designs and Patents Act 1988.

*All rights reserved. No part of this publication may be reproduced, stored in a retrieval system,
or transmitted in any form or by any means, electronic, mechanical, photocopying, recording or
otherwise, without the prior permission of the publisher or a licence permitting restricted copying.
In the UK such licences are issued by the Copyright Licensing Agency,
90 Tottenham Court Road, London W1P 9HE.*

British Library Cataloguing in Publication Data
A catalogue record for this book is available from the British Library

ISBN 1-84227-133-4
Unless otherwise stated, Scripture quotations are taken from the
Library of Congress Cataloging-in-Publication Data

Rome in the Bible and the early church / edited by Peter Oakes.
    p. cm.
  Includes bibliographical references.
  ISBN 0-8010-2608-3 (paper)
    1. Bible. N.T.—Criticism, interpretation, etc. 2. Rome in the Bible. 3. Church
history—Primitive and early church, ca. 30-600. I. Oakes, Peter (Peter S.)

BS2545.R65 R66 2002
274.5'63201—dc21   2002023060

HOLY BIBLE, NEW INTERNATIONAL VERSION
Copyright © 1973, 1978, 1984 by the International Bible Society.
Used by permission of Hodder and Stoughton Limited. All rights reserved.
'NIV' is a registered trademark of the International Bible Society
UK trademark number 1448790

Cover Design by FourNineZero
Typeset by WestKey Ltd, Falmouth, Cornwall
Printed in Great Britain by Bell & Bain, Glasgow

JESUIT - KRAUSS - McCORMICK - LIBRARY
1100 EAST 55th STREET
CHICAGO, ILLINOIS 60615

Contents

Contributors

Andrew D. Clarke, Lecturer in New Testament Studies, University of Aberdeen.

Conrad Gempf, Lecturer in New Testament Studies, London Bible College.

Andrew Gregory, Chaplain and Oakeshott Junior Research Fellow, Lincoln College, Oxford.

Peter Oakes, Greenwood Lecturer in New Testament Studies, University of Manchester.

Steve Walton, Lecturer in Greek and New Testament Studies, London Bible College.

Bruce Winter, Director, Institute for Early Christianity in the Graeco-Roman World, Tyndale House, Cambridge.

Preface

As the noise dies down from the Oscars ceremony that turned into a celebration of the film *Gladiator* (and as cheekily enlarged frames from it appear, showing gas bottles on the backs of chariots!), it seems a good time to reflect on how the New Testament and the earliest churches related to Rome, both as a power and as the location of an important church. One reason why we need to do this is to minimise the number of gas bottles, or figures in blue jeans, that slip into our study of the Bible. Another, broader, reason is that the New Testament and early post-Apostolic texts were written in, and primarily for, a certain context: to understand them, we need to examine them in that context.

But, as you can feel from its weight, this is not an encyclopaedic book about first-century culture – other books handle that well. Instead, a group of writers committed to both history and theology tackle six issues covering a good range of the areas in which the Bible and the early church relate to Rome. How does Luke-Acts relate to the Roman empire? Why does Luke give us such a surprising account of Paul's arrival at Rome? How does the ethical section of Paul's letter to the Romans relate to Roman culture? Why does Paul give such a long list of greetings to different types of Christians at Rome? How does Paul write about the Roman authorities when he is a prisoner himself and is writing to the suffering church at Philippi? Can scholars justify making generalisations about the development of the church at Rome on the basis of *1 Clement*?

The book grew out of the 1999 meeting of the Tyndale Fellowship New Testament Study Group in Cambridge. I would like to thank Peter Head for organising the conference and Howard

Marshall for chairing it. Particular thanks are due to Kevin Ellis for co-editing the early stages of this project. Thanks are also due to Tony Graham and the team at Paternoster for accepting and working on the book. And many thanks to Janet, both for word-processing and for patient support through the book's development.

Peter Oakes
Easter 2001

Abbreviations

A1CS   Bruce Winter (ed.), *The Book of Acts in its First Century Setting*, 6 vols. (Grand Rapids: Eerdmans / Carlisle: Paternoster, 1993)

AB   Anchor Bible

ABD   D.N. Freedman (ed.), The *Anchor Bible Dictionary* (New York: Doubleday, 1992)

ABRL   Anchor Bible Reference Library

AGJU   Arbeiten zur Geschichte des antiken Judentums und des Urchristentums

AnBib   Analecta biblica

ANRW   H. Temporini and W. Haase (eds.), *Aufstieg und Niedergang der römischen Welt: Geschichte und Kultur Roms im Spiegel der neueren Forschung* (Berlin: W. de Gruyter, 1972–)

BDAG   W. Bauer, F.W. Danker, W.F. Arndt and F.W. Gingrich (eds.), *A Greek–English Lexicon of the New Testament and Other Early Christian Literature* (Chicago: University of Chicago Press, 2000³)

BETL   Bibliotheca ephemeridum theologicarum lovaniensium

Bib   *Biblica*

BR   *Bible Review*

CBQMS   *Catholic Biblical Quarterly*, Monograph Series

CIL   *Corpus inscriptionum latinarum*

HDR   Harvard Dissertations in Religion

HTR   *Harvard Theological Review*

ICC   International Critical Commentary

IGRR	R. Cagnat (ed.), *Inscriptiones graecae ad res romanas pertinentes*, 3 vols. (Paris: Leroux, 1911–27)
ILS	H. Dessau (ed.), *Inscriptionaes latinae selectae*
JBR	*Journal of Bible and Religion*
JRS	*Journal of Roman Studies*
JSNT	*Journal for the Study of the New Testament*
JSNTSup	*Journal for the Study of the New Testament*, Supplement Series
JSOTSup	*Journal for the Study of the Old Testament*, Supplement Series
JTS	*Journal of Theological Studies*
LSJ	H.G. Liddell, R. Scott, H.S. Jones and R. McKenzie (eds.), *A Greek–English Lexicon*, 2 vols. (Oxford: Clarendon Press, 1951⁹)
MM	J.H. Moulton and G. Milligan, *The Vocabulary of the Greek Testament Illustrated from the Papyri and Other Non-Literary Sources* (London: Hodder & Stoughton, 1930)
NAC	New American Commentary
NICNT	New International Commentary on the New Testament
NIGTC	The New International Greek Testament Commentary
NovT	Novum Testamentum
NTD	Das Neue Testament Deutsch
NTS	*New Testament Studies*
OGIS	W. Dittenberger (ed.), *Orientis Graeci Inscriptiones Selectae*, 2 vols. (Lipsiae: S. Hirzel, 1903–05)
PBSR	*Papers of the British School at Rome*
RTR	*Reformed Theological Review*
SBLDS	Society of Biblical Literature Dissertation Series
SBLMS	Society of Biblical Literature Monograph Series
SBLSP	Society of Biblical Literature Seminar Papers
SEG	*Supplementum Epigraphicum Graecum*
SJT	*Scottish Journal of Theology*
SNTSMS	Society for New Testament Studies Monograph Series
StPatr	*Studia Patristica*
TAPA	*Transactions of the American Philological Association*

TNTC	Tyndale New Testament Commentaries
TynBul	*Tyndale Bulletin*
WBC	Word Biblical Commentary
WUNT	Wissenschaftliche Untersuchungen zum Neuen Testament
ZNW	*Zeitschrift für die neutestamentliche Wissenschaft*
ZTK	*Zeitschrift für Theologie und Kirche*

Introduction

Rome has meant many things to many people. But what about the earliest Christians, in the first century after Christ's ministry – what did it mean for them? In this book, chapters by six writers pick up on six ways in which this question ought to be answered.

The answers fall into two types because Rome both dominated the shape of first-century life and became a place of Christian activity. So, Rome was an empire in which Christians lived. Rome was an authority under which they might suffer. Rome was a culture expressed in life in society. On the other hand, Rome was the location of a church. It was a church to which Paul wrote and the first church naming itself in its writings. Finally, Rome was the place to which Paul was taken at the end of his ministry, as recorded in the Book of Acts.

The six writers seek to move scholarship forward in each of these six areas. However, it is not only to scholars that this book should be of interest. For anyone who studies the New Testament, it is important to reflect on how it works within its first-century setting. For many New Testament texts this means primarily looking at their Graeco-Roman context and, while Greece supplies the language and many underlying cultural assumptions, it is Rome that dominates first-century life and, for some texts, provides a specific location. In addition to the New Testament texts, we have included two from outside the canon, *1 Clement* and the *Shepherd of Hermas*. These play an important role in discussion of what the early church in Rome was like.

Rome was an empire. In the New Testament we see the empire most at work as we read Luke's Gospel and the Book of Acts.

Scholars have repeatedly wrestled with the question of whether Luke is deliberately saying something about the Roman empire. Steve Walton enters this discussion by assessing the strengths and limitations of current approaches and then making his own proposal, that Luke 'offers his readers a strategy of critical distance from the empire'.[1] What Walton means is that Luke deliberately offers a variety of perspectives on the empire, both positive and negative. Luke shows that relationships with the authorities can be positive. His readers are to make use of that, respect it, seek to maintain it, and even try to persuade the authorities back to it if things turn sour. And they may turn sour. In such a case, Christians must be willing to maintain a faithful witness even though, as Luke shows, it may result in death. The Christians can be confident of their final vindication, both because Christ was vindicated and because, ultimately, Christ, not Caesar, is lord, king and saviour. God is working out his purposes through the Christian community and the empire may help or seek to hinder, but God's plans will come to fruition.

Staying with Luke, one important New Testament answer to the question 'What is Rome?' is that it is the place at which the Book of Acts ends. This is a far from trivial point, especially given the issues that Walton deals with in his chapter. Luke takes Acts from Jerusalem to Rome. But what does he do when it gets there? The brief answer is, 'None of the things anyone expects him to'. Conrad Gempf looks at the surprising account in Acts 28 of Paul's arrival at and time in Rome, and asks what Luke is trying to say. Gempf's study of 28:14–28 looks at the structure of the narrative and at Luke's tightly focused set of characters. The structure is seen to exclude the suggestion that Luke's aim is to present Paul as the pioneer of Roman evangelism. Instead, a careful analysis of the presentation of the characters, especially as seen in their speeches, shows that the interest is in the complex relationship between Paul and the Roman Jews. The Jews come to an imprisoned fellow Jew, who then announces his Roman credentials but asserts that he is no threat to the Jewish community at Rome. Rather, his imprisonment is for the Jewish cause. The Roman Jews respond with great circumspection and will not pose a threat to him. In fact, they would like to hear him speak because they know little about the Jewish group of which he is part.

---

[1] Walton, p. 35 below.

In Luke's Rome, Jews do know of Christians. They may have heard only bad things about the group but they still see them as a part of Judaism and remain interested and willing to talk. There is some sort of 'parting of the ways', responsibility for which Luke places on the Jews. However, bad feeling between Jews and Christians is not as violent as might be expected, given many scholars' reading of the riots reported by Suetonius. This also raises issues of the relationship between Luke's view and what was actually happening in Rome. Gempf points out that the rather nervous 'posturing' that goes on in the interchange between Paul and the Jews actually sits well with what we know of the insecurity of the Jewish community at Rome. However, Gempf's main interest is a narrative one. The narrative is seen as a subtle presentation of issues both of connection and of disconnection between Christianity and Judaism.

Rome was a culture, with a pattern of society intimately bound up with a system of laws. Bruce Winter argues that in Romans 12–15 Paul is 'a radical critic of the prevailing culture of privilege in Rome's society'.[2] Paul repeatedly calls for action that contravenes social expectations. He resists the idea that Christians should behave according to the three expected patterns of social interaction: patron–client relations, relations between (unequal) friends, and the ways in which associations conducted themselves. Instead, Paul scandalously extends the scope of family language to cover the relationships in the Christian community.

In Romans 12 this works out first in a rejection of status as determinant of role. Instead, roles within the community depend on the will of God and the measure of faith, not rank. Paul then forbids the Christians to use the status-based means of redress, the law-courts, for difficulties that they face. Where Roman society expected legal action, the Christians should rely on God's judgement and should seek the good of those who troubled them. In 13:1–7 Paul does encourage the positive cultural phenomenon of public benefaction (13:3). Winter argues that, ironically, the instruction to pay taxes is counter-cultural. The prevailing culture in the late 50s was of antagonism to paying taxes because there had been much controversy over them. The call to avoid being under obligation to anyone (13:8) is more obviously contrary to Roman

---

[2] Winter, p. 99, below.

culture because the fabric of society was a complex network of sustained obligations. The attack on promiscuity (13:13–14) carries social significance because such behaviour was primarily expected of privileged men. Finally, the call for the 'strong' to amend their behaviour for the sake of the interests of the 'weak' (14:1–15:13) works radically against the norms of society in which the interests of the strong – the patron, the higher-status friend, the senior members of the association – always dictated the course of events. Throughout Romans 12–15 Paul calls for behaviour that is the antithesis to Roman social and legal expectations.

Andrew Clarke effectively reinforces this counter-cultural emphasis with a study of Romans 16. He uses Galatians 3.28 ('There is neither Jew nor Greek, neither slave nor free, neither male nor female, for you are all one in Christ Jesus') as a grid for surveying Paul's list of greetings to the Christian community in Rome. Clarke shows how each dimension of the inclusiveness of Galatians 3:28 – ethnic, social and gender – is exemplified in the construction of the list of greetings. He shows that Paul transcends these three key boundary distinctions of Graeco-Roman society, not only in a polemical argument such as Galatians 3, but also in his relations with the church at Rome and, indeed, elsewhere. What at first seems simply a list actually conveys a substantial theological point.

Clarke's analysis inevitably draws on Peter Lampe's work on Romans 16. However, Clarke uses and evaluates a range of other evidence and arguments, which make his chapter a useful contribution to study of the social composition of the church at Rome. However, Clarke's own essential point is that Paul's inclusive theology, seen not only in Galatians but in the main theological argument in Romans 1–15, is presented in the list of greetings too.

I would also suggest a further implication of Clarke's chapter. As he notes, the passage is directed to 'the Christian congregation located in the heart of the Roman empire'.[3] I think that Paul might wish to exemplify at length, in a letter sent to Rome itself, the point that Eberhard Faust makes for Ephesians 2: that it is Christ, not the Roman emperor and the empire, that can bring

---

[3] Clarke, p. 108, below.

inter-ethnic peace.[4] Following from Clarke's analysis, Paul's point would go beyond the purely ethnic one. In Romans 16 Paul presents Christ as bringing harmony across ethnic, status and gender divisions. Christ unifies in a way that Rome cannot.

Another aspect of Rome was as a system of authority: central authority embodied in the emperor and localised authorities backed by the power of the centre. My own chapter in this collection explores Paul's response to this in Philippians. He is forced up against this aspect of Rome because he is imprisoned and faces possible execution. Moreover, he is writing to the Christians at Philippi who are themselves suffering. As we would expect, Paul tells the Philippians about his imprisonment. But what he chooses to tell them about it is very unexpected. He writes of progress for the gospel among the Praetorian Guard, then about Christians preaching in order to stir up trouble for him in prison. He writes about his possible execution, then about his certainty of release. How do these fit together? A common theme seems to be the sovereignty of the gospel over every aspect of his imprisonment. Such a theme then also forms a link with material elsewhere in the letter about Christ's universal sovereignty and his triumphant return. That material is shaped in such a way as to evoke comparison with Rome and to assert Christ's sovereignty over it. The imprisonment passage and the texts about Christ can be related together if we see both as expressions of Paul's reaction to the Roman authorities. Paul and the Philippians can be confident and stand firm in their difficult situations because, both in Paul's imprisonment and in Christ's triumph, God is sovereign over the Roman authorities.

Turning to the final chapter in the book, if we look at the Christian community in Rome, we are compelled by recent scholarship to move beyond the New Testament canon. It has become standard for scholars to use Paul's letter to the Romans as the starting point of a process, which is then traced through New Testament books that may have been written in Rome and whose end lies in some of the post-Apostolic texts originating from

---

[4] E. Faust, *Pax Christi et Pax Caesaris: Religionsgeschichtliche, traditions-geschichtliche u. Sozialgeschichtliche Studien zum Epheserbrief* (Freiburg: Universitätsverlag / Göttingen: Vandenhoeck & Ruprecht, 1993).

Rome. *1 Clement* is always used; sometimes there is also *Shepherd of Hermas* and, occasionally, the works of Justin Martyr.

The traced path becomes a 'trajectory' of the development of the early Roman church. Usually, the trajectory is seen in terms of a process of change from an originally radical, charismatic and creative community to a socially conformist, institutional hierarchy on its way to becoming the dominant force in the Christian church as a whole.

Andrew Gregory questions the basis of the trajectory. He first shows the difficulty of closely dating either *1 Clement* or *Shepherd*. This difficulty is so great as to make it unclear which text is the earlier. He then argues that it is difficult to infer a great deal about Roman Christianity from the texts. Finally, he points out that even with the conventional scholarly scheme, in which *1 Clement* precedes *Shepherd*, the trajectory is disturbed because the 'institutional' *1 Clement* is followed by *Shepherd*, in which the 'charismatic' and the 'institutional' sit together.

Gregory argues ultimately for a move away from studying these texts predominantly in relation to the city of Rome. He prefers to see them in terms of Roman culture more widely. An important effect of this is to stress the value of studying what Roman Christianity had in common with other Christian communities, rather than following the current trend towards almost exclusive interest in what was distinctive to each community.

Rome: city, empire, authority, culture: in both Rome's narrower and wider senses it is a context in which early Christianity took root and in which key texts were produced. Some texts react to Rome; others challenge Rome's values; yet others express the life of the Christian community that grew in Rome. As Luke goes to pains to point out, the founding of Christianity happened at a period defined by Roman authority. Exploring the interaction between the texts and Rome must always be an important element of the study of the New Testament and the early church.

The State They Were in: Luke's View of the Roman Empire[1]

Steve Walton

Scholars have long debated Luke's view of the Roman empire – and for good reasons. Luke's Jesus is silent in the face of his accusers before the Roman procurator Pontius Pilate, but in similar situations Luke's Paul speaks up for himself and claims his rights as a Roman citizen. Luke alone records that Jesus had a Zealot among his disciples, but he portrays the early Christians as non-violent and compliant in the face of a sometimes-hostile state. Luke presents the Jewish authorities as responsible for the death of Jesus, but also implicates the Roman empire in Jesus' demise by characterising Pilate as weak and ineffectual. Further, this is no mere academic debate, for similar tensions can be seen in Christian responses throughout history to nation-states whose attitudes vary from out-right hostility through undermining by absorption to modern western pluralism.

Within the New Testament there is a range of views of the state, from Paul's apparently positive and 'submissive' view (Rom. 13:1–7) through 1 Peter's concern to witness by being ready to suffer for doing right (3:13–17; cf. 2:13–17; 4:12–15) to the seer's vision of the same Roman state as the beast that rises from the sea to oppose the

[1] Previous rescensions of this chapter were presented at the New Testament research seminar of London Bible College and the Acts seminar of the British New Testament Conference (Roehampton, September 2000). Prof. Edwin Judge and Drs Bruce Winter, David Gill and Gerald Borchert kindly advised me or commented on partial or full drafts. I am grateful to all of them; inadequacies that remain are, of course, my own responsibility.

people of God (Rev. 13). Presumably these varying approaches reflect the various situations of the writers and their readers. So where does Luke fit on this spectrum? In this chapter I shall briefly outline major views in scholarship before discussing key passages and themes in Luke-Acts, and critiquing the main views in the light of this examination. Finally, I shall propose a series of theses summarising Luke's view of how Christians should see the Roman state.

Previous Views

Five key views can be found in scholarship of the last two hundred years. The first is by far the dominant view until recent times; the last thirty years have seen a growth in alternative perspectives, reflecting the decline in the dominance of historical-critical scholarship and the growth of other methods of reading the New Testament. The proposals are that (1) Luke-Acts is a political apology on behalf of the church addressed to Roman officials; (2) Luke-Acts is an apology on behalf of the Roman state addressed to the church;[2] (3) Luke-Acts is providing legitimation for the church's identity; (4) Acts is equipping the church to live with the Roman empire; and (5) Luke-Acts is not interested in politics at all.

Political apology for the church to Rome

This approach has the claim to age, for it can be traced back to the work of Heumann in the eighteenth century.[3] In recent times it finds classic statements in the work of Easton, Cadbury, Conzelmann and Bruce.[4] While particular emphases differ – often considerably – these

---

[2] Klaus Wengst, *Pax Romana and the Peace of Jesus Christ*, 89–105, seeks to combine these first two views by arguing that Luke's intended readership includes Christians, sympathisers and non-Christians. His basis for this claim is that the dedications of Luke and Acts imply that Theophilus is to see that the books are published (101), but this demonstrates little about the intended readership of the volumes.

[3] C.A. Heumann, 'Dissertatio de Theophilo, cui Lucas historiam sacram inscripsit', 483–505, cited by W.W. Gasque, *A History of the Criticism of the Acts of the Apostles*, 21–2; Philip F. Esler, *Community and Gospel in Luke-Acts*, 205.

scholars agree that Luke is offering an apologetic designed to persuade Roman officials that Christianity is politically harmless. Many also believe that Luke is seeking to show that Christianity should be regarded as a subspecies of Judaism, in order that Christians may receive the same freedom to practise their faith that the Roman empire afforded to Jews.[5] This latter point is usually expressed by claiming that Luke wishes Christianity to be seen as a *religio licita* (a 'legally-recognised' religion).[6]

For Conzelmann (and some – but not all – others), coming to terms with the empire is part of the reality of dealing with the delay of the parousia; Luke needs to help his church adjust to issues that could in earlier times be glossed over (and hence, e.g., Paul in Rom. 13:1ff. takes a positive view of the empire, for he wrote in a period of 'imminent expectation'). Thus Luke's use of 'apology' language (particularly ἀπολογέομαι and ἀπολογία[7]) indicates the purpose of his account.

---

[4] Burton Scott Easton, *Early Christianity*, 42–57; Henry J. Cadbury, *The Making of Luke-Acts*, 308–15; Hans Conzelmann, *The Theology of St Luke*, 137–49; F.F. Bruce, *The Book of Acts*, 8–13; also Harry W. Tajra, *The Trial of St Paul*, 199; Robert F. O'Toole, SJ, 'Luke's Position on Politics and Society in Luke-Acts', 1–17, citing 4–8.

[5] Easton, *Early Christianity*, 46, observes that Luke uses αἵρεσις for the church (Acts 24:5; 28:22) as well as for the Pharisaic and Sadducean Jewish parties (Acts 5:17; 15:5; 26:5).

[6] E.g. ibid. 43. This phrase appears to be used in ancient literature only by Tertullian, *Apology* 21.1. Hans Conzelmann, *Acts of the Apostles*, xlvii, distances himself from this specific view, observing correctly that Luke does not argue on the basis of Roman law; cf. in agreement, Henry J. Cadbury, 'Some Foibles of New Testament Scholarship', 213–16, 215 – failing to admit that he himself defends the idea that Luke is arguing that Christianity should be legally recognised in his earlier work (Cadbury, *Making*, 308–15)! This is not to deny that Judaism had a particular place in the empire (see Josephus, *Antiquities* 14.186–285 = 14.10.1–11.4; 16.160–74 = 16.6.1–8, and the valuable discussion in Tajra, *Trial of St Paul*, 14–21), but simply to assert that there was not a general Roman legal category of *religio licita* into which Christianity might fit.

[7] The verb is found in Acts 19:33; 24:10; 25:8; 26:1, 2, 24 (cf. Luke 12:11; 21:14); the noun, in Acts 22:1; 25:16. These are Lukanisms not found in the other Gospels, and only occurring eight times in the rest of the New Testament.

This apology is accomplished by two main strategies. First, Luke shows that whenever Roman officials consider the case of Christians (in particular, Paul) or Jesus, they are found innocent of political wrongdoing. Second, Luke portrays the attitudes of these Roman officials towards the Christians as positive.

Thus in Acts examples include that the first Gentile convert is the centurion Cornelius (10:1 – 11:18); Sergius Paulus, the governor of Cyprus, believes (13:12); the Philippian praetors apologise to Paul and Silas when they realise they have acted wrongly (16:39); the Thessalonian politarchs simply put the missionaries' host Jason on bail, rather than acting against Paul, Silas and Timothy (17:9); in Corinth the proconsul Gallio rejects the accusations against Paul as internal Jewish debates (18:14–16); the Ephesian Asiarchs seek to protect Paul, and the town clerk rejects the uproar over Paul's ministry (19:31, 35–41); Claudius Lysias rescues Paul and writes that he is innocent (21:31–2, 37–40; 23:29); Felix pays no attention to Tertullus's indictment of Paul as an insurrectionist (24:5–6, 22) and treats Paul well (24:23–7); Festus tells Agrippa that Paul is innocent of political charges (25:25) and Agrippa agrees (26:32); and on arrival in Rome Paul is allowed to live in his own rented place and to preach freely (28:30–1).

Further, in Luke's Gospel Jesus is declared innocent by Pilate three times (23:4, 13–14, 22), by the Roman client-king Herod (23:15), and by the centurion at the foot of the cross (23:47).[8] By contrast, Luke emphasises the responsibility of the Jewish leaders for the death of Jesus (Luke 23:1–2, 5, 10, 18, 21, 23, 25, 35; Acts 2:23; 3:14; 4:11; 7:52; 10:39; 13:27–8),[9] and presents the Jews as the cause of civil disturbance when Paul visits towns and cities (Acts 13:50; 14:5, 19; 17:5–7, 13; 18:12–13; 21:27–9; 22:22–3) and

---

[8] Each of these Gospel passages is either without parallel in, or shows a different wording from, the other synoptic evangelists.

[9] Again, many of the Gospel passages represent Lukan *Sondergut*. Jack T. Sanders, *The Jews in Luke-Acts*, presents the evidence fully, although note the effective critique of his conclusions by Jon A. Weatherly, *Jewish Responsibility for the Death of Jesus in Luke-Acts*, and Jon A. Weatherly, 'The Jews in Luke-Acts', 107–17, arguing cogently that Luke presents the responsibility for the death of Jesus as lying with the Jews *of Jerusalem* rather than all Jews everywhere; thus Sanders misrepresents Luke as anti-Semitic.

as the ones who pursue the (false) accusations against him
(Acts 23:12–15; 24:1–6; 25:1–3, 7).

Apology for Rome to the church

A second proposal is that Luke is writing to persuade his Christian
readers of his own positive view of the Roman empire in the light
of Christians who are either suspicious of it (Walaskay) or courting
(semi-deliberate) martyrdom (Maddox[10]). A common feature of
scholars espousing this view is their rejection of the claim that Luke
is writing for a non-Christian audience and the repeated quotation
of Barrett's famous verdict concerning the 'political apology' view:
'No Roman official would ever have filtered out so much of what
to him would be theological and ecclesiastical rubbish in order to
reach so tiny a grain of relevant apology. So far as Acts was an
apology, it was an apology addressed to the Church ....'[11]

Walaskay argues cogently that there are features of Luke's presentation of the empire that do not fit the 'political apology' view so
well and fit this view better.[12] In particular he identifies elements in
Luke-Acts that would be disturbing or unhelpful in persuading a
Roman official of the harmlessness of Christianity: Jesus has a
Zealot among his disciples (Luke 6:15, contrast Mark 3:18; Acts
1:13); Jesus commands his followers to buy swords (Luke 22:35–8);
the emphasis on Jesus as Lord and king throughout Luke-Acts
would sit uncomfortably with the use of these titles for Caesar;
and the silence of the ending of Acts would not impress a Roman
official reading the book, for such a reader would not have been
shown that Paul was innocent.

Walaskay also responds to the claim that there are features of
Luke-Acts' presentation of the empire that portray imperial power
as capricious, harsh or corrupt (see below, pp. 19–20, 23–5).
Walaskay's response to these elements is to claim that Luke constantly presents the various Roman magistrates as under pressure

---

[10] Robert Maddox, *The Purpose of Luke-Acts*, 96–7, noting particularly
the evidence of 1 Pet. 2:13–17 as suggesting that this tendency developed
quite early in the life of the church.
[11] C.K. Barrett, *Luke the Historian in Recent Study*, 63.
[12] Paul W. Walaskay, *And So We Came to Rome*, esp. 15–37.

from jealous Jews, and to suggest that Luke is showing the durability of the imperial legal system.[13]

Walaskay observes that Luke does not present the kind of anti-Roman polemic found in *4 Esdras,* the *Sibylline Oracles* (bk. 8) and Revelation; rather Luke glosses over negative aspects of the empire and presents imperial power positively. Thus Jesus' birth is placed in the context of the empire (Luke 2:1–5), showing that God's plan of salvation is being worked out in conjunction with the empire's history: the *pax Augusta* would be completed by the *pax Christi.* John's preaching reflects Augustan ideals of fair taxes and just military rule (Luke 3:10–14). Luke often presents centurions and other Roman officials positively.[14] He has edited Mark's story of the question concerning tribute to Caesar (Mark 12:13–17; Luke 20:20–6) to heighten the treachery of the Jewish leaders (note v. 20); Luke's purpose in including this story is to answer Christians who were unsure about paying tribute to Caesar – the question would have seemed a non-question to a Roman official, for it was obvious that such tribute should be paid! Luke has edited Mark 10:42–5 and inserted it into the Last Supper narrative (Luke 22:24–7) in order to portray the empire more favourably (see further below, pp. 19–20).

Walaskay follows this with a point-by-point discussion of the trials of Jesus and Paul.[15] He claims that Luke presents Pilate as dealing fairly with Jesus and maintaining his innocence, whereas the sinful Jewish leaders pervert justice in order to do away with Jesus. Paul defends himself by appeal to the resurrection of Jesus, and thereby shows Christians of Luke's day both that their predecessors were innocent before the state and that Paul had no political quarrel with Rome.

Robbins's view is close to those of Walaskay and Maddox, although more nuanced, for he argues that Luke-Acts is commending a symbiotic relationship between the empire and Christianity.[16] He believes that Luke-Acts is intended to support Christians building strategic alliances with local leaders in the

---

[13] Ibid. 23–5.

[14] Luke 7:2; 23:47; Acts 10:1ff.; 22:25–6; 23:17, 23; 27:1ff.; 28:16.

[15] Walaskay, *And So We Came,* 39–63.

[16] Vernon K. Robbins, 'Luke-Acts', 202–21.

Roman empire (and thus is written for a Christian audience). Robbins identifies a number of ways in which the church works in similar manner to the empire: different levels of workers operate, negotiation happens with insiders and outsiders, both develop a presence everywhere, and both extend citizenship to new groups. The eastern empire is the 'workplace' of Christianity: it is where power 'takes place', particularly in synagogues and homes. Jesus' followers are in an analogous position to those in the Roman military system, for they have no choice but to do God's work. God ensures that his will is communicated and executed by using angels, the Lord Jesus and the Spirit at key moments, to work through and with obedient Christian leaders.

Legitimation

Esler rejects both apologetic views and proposes that Luke is writing for a Christian audience and offering them legitimation for their beliefs and lifestyle, which includes assurance that faith in Christ is not incompatible with allegiance to Rome.[17] He is rightly critical of the *religio licita* theory, on the ground that we know nothing of such a category in the first century AD, as well as rejecting Walaskay's view, since Luke's portrayal of the relationship of Rome and Christianity is mixed, including situations in which Roman officials treat Jesus and Paul unfairly or badly.

Esler draws attention to the presentation of Christianity as an ancestral religion in order to help legitimate his readers' beliefs by appealing to the (Roman) cultural value of antiquity – the supposed 'new' religion was in fact ancient. Thus Luke omits 'new' from his Markan source (Mark 1:27; Luke 4:36), he adds 'the old is best' (Luke 5:39; contrast Mark 2:22), and he regards the Athenians' love of new things as scornful (Acts 17:19, 21). Further, Luke repeatedly links Christianity with Israelite ancestors (Acts 3:13; 5:30; 15:10; 22:14; 26:6; 28:25).

Esler proposes that within Luke's community there were a number of Roman soldiers or administrators who needed

---

[17] Esler, *Community and Gospel in Luke-Acts*, 201–19; so also Ben Witherington III, *The Acts of the Apostles*, 810–11; Helen K. Bond, *Pontius Pilate in History and Interpretation*, 161–2.

reassurance that Christian faith and serving the empire could coexist satisfactorily. He claims that Luke diverges from his sources to highlight such Romans among the first believers, including the centurions (Luke 7:1–10; 23:47; Acts 10:1ff.[18]), Sergius Paulus (Acts 13:6–12), and Titius Justus (Acts 18:7). Further, Luke adds ethical advice to soldiers and tax-collectors in his account of John's preaching (Luke 3:12–14), and gives prominence to Paul claiming his rights as a Roman citizen (Acts 16:37–40; 22:25–9).

However, this is hardly 'quite a body of evidence';[19] it simply involves the doubtful procedure of 'mirror-reading'[20] Luke-Acts for its audience. Of course the contents and presentation of a book will tell us *something* about the intended audience; Mark's explanation of Jewish washing customs (Mark 7:3–4) suggests that he does not expect his readers to know about them. However, to argue that the presence of these features implies a significant presence of Romans in Luke's church assumes both that Luke is

---

[18] Esler, *Community and Gospel in Luke-Acts*, 95–6, argues that the account of Cornelius's conversion is unhistorical on the grounds that (1) for Peter subsequently to do the about-face described in Gal. 2:11–14 is incredible; (2) we should not expect Peter to be the 'apostle to the circumcised' and Paul the 'apostle to the uncircumcised' if it had been Peter who began the Gentile mission; (3) we should expect that the Council (Acts 15) would simply refer back to this event *as decisive* if it were historical. However: (1) Peter is presented as changing his behaviour in different company (particularly when under pressure) in the Gospels, including in Luke (esp. 22:54–62); (2) the titles in Galatians are concerned with the *focus* of the two apostles' ministry – one could equally argue (equally erroneously, that is) that Paul should be known as 'apostle to the circumcised', on the basis that he constantly goes to synagogues in Acts; (3) the use of ἡσύκασαν (11:18) need not imply acceptance, as in Luke 14:4; Acts 21:14 (the only other use of the verb in Acts) it may well imply continuing reservations, such reservations only being resolved at the Council (James D.G. Dunn, *The Acts of the Apostles*, 152). In any case the question in 11:1–18 is about the acceptance of Peter eating with this group of Gentiles, and does not raise the question of whether circumcision was required for Gentile converts, which is the central question in 15:1ff.

[19] Esler, *Community and Gospel in Luke-Acts*, 210.

[20] For the phrase, see John M.G. Barclay, 'Mirror-reading a Polemical Letter', 73–93.

writing for a particular, identifiable, small community (a claim Bauckham has rightly challenged[21]) and that each feature in Luke-Acts corresponds to a need or grouping within Luke's church – an assumption that needs only to be stated in order to see that it is unlikely to be correct. In any case, as we have seen, the presentation of Roman officials is rather more mixed than Esler's brief presentation allows, and Luke-Acts presents Jesus, rather than Caesar, as Lord and king.

Equipping

Cassidy offers a further level of nuancing of Luke's presentation of the empire, which seeks to take greater account of the 'mixed message' that appears to come through in Luke-Acts.[22] Like Esler he rejects 'apologetic' explanations of Luke's presentation of the empire, arguing that Acts does not present Christians as politically harmless or law-abiding, for there are a large number of public controversies concerning Christianity, particularly featuring Paul. When he arrives in a city his preaching frequently leads to public disorder, causing him to have to leave. Cassidy argues that Luke does not show that the problems were due to Jewish troublemakers, for the problems only arose when Paul came into a city. Further, Paul is not finally exonerated by Roman justice; for example, in the case of Gallio Paul simply benefits from bias against the Jews.

Indeed, Cassidy notes, Paul's attitude to his Roman citizenship and his co-operation with Roman officials are highly qualified in Acts. Although Paul is generally co-operative, he is hardly an unquestioningly loyal Roman citizen: he identifies himself as a citizen of Tarsus (Acts 21:39); he mentions his citizenship only in private to officials who fail to treat him properly; and Paul's references to Jesus as 'Lord' show that he does not see Caesar as exercising ultimate sovereignty (cf. Acts 17:7). In places Paul is far

---

[21] Richard Bauckham (ed.), *The Gospels for All Christians*; see Esler's review and Bauckham's rejoinder: Philip F. Esler, 'Community and Gospel in Early Christianity', 235–48; Richard Bauckham, 'Response to Philip Esler', 249–53.

[22] Richard J. Cassidy, *Society and Politics in the Acts of the Apostles*, esp. 145–70; cf. Richard J. Cassidy, *Jesus, Politics, and Society*.

from accommodating to his judges: he speaks with Felix of 'justice, self-control, and the coming judgement' (Acts 24:25), and rebukes Festus (Acts 25:10). Luke portrays Paul as not expecting to receive justice from Festus; that is why he reacts angrily and appeals to Caesar (Acts 25:10–11), and tells the Roman Jews that he was *compelled* (ἠναγκάσθην) to appeal to Caesar (Acts 28:19).

Cassidy asserts that Luke does not in fact portray the Roman empire particularly favourably, for Paul was in prison for four years without an effective verdict, principally because of corrupt judges (Acts 24:26, 27; 25:9). Christians are pictured as those who are critical of human authority, for they have a higher allegiance (Acts 4:19–20; 5:29).

Thus Cassidy proposes a threefold theory of Luke's purposes, which he calls the 'allegiance-conduct-witness' theory: he wrote to share and express his own faith in Jesus, to provide his fellow Christians with guidance how to live under Roman rule, and to give guidance and perspective for Christians when on trial before political authorities. The first is relatively uncontroversial; the second and third, Cassidy believes, show why Luke presents the trials of Jesus and Paul as he does. Luke is demonstrating that faithful witness is required in such situations, but different outcomes might come from trials – severe punishment and even death were real possibilities.

In particular, Cassidy cites Luke's editing of Mark 13:9–13 in Luke 21:12–19 as showing that Jesus is here giving significantly fuller guidance to disciples:[23] he speaks of disciples experiencing betrayal by family and even death (21:16); he gives more definite advice on how to act when on trial (21:14–15); 21:12 shows greater emphasis on secular persecution, for he places 'kings' first, adds 'prisons' and omits Mark's 'councils'; the addition of 'before all this' (21:12) shows that the instructions are for a time before the cataclysmic upheavals to come.

Cassidy also argues that his view fits the ending of Acts better than others, for it shows the book climaxing with Paul ready to testify before Caesar. Luke thereby encourages his readers to be faithful in their own testimony to Jesus in 'ordinary' life.

---

[23] Cassidy, *Society and Politics in Acts*, 165 (with n. 18).

Thus, Cassidy asserts, five concerns animated Luke in writing.[24] Luke wished (1) to inform his readers both about Jesus' trials before Roman officials and his predictions that his disciples would have similar experiences; (2) to equip his readers to handle such trials rightly by presenting Jesus' instructions on what to do; (3) to make his audience aware that some leading disciples had, in fact, suffered such trials; (4) to warn his readers of the different possible trial outcomes, which might include death or imprisonment; (5) to encourage his readers to show the same faithfulness of testimony when under trial as Jesus and the leading disciples.

Not interested in politics

Finally, Jervell and Franklin argue that Luke is simply uninterested in the politics of the Roman empire.[25] Franklin sees Luke's focus as being on the triumph of God in Paul's arrival in Rome; Roman officials are merely agents used by God to achieve his purposes. Luke is not favourable towards the empire, for he presents Pilate unfavourably (Luke 23:13–25; 13:1), he includes sayings that predict the destruction of the temple by Rome (Luke 23:28–31), he shows the empire acting badly towards Christians (Acts 16:39; 17:6–10; 18:12–17), and he shows the Roman authorities as uncomprehending of Christian preaching (Acts 24:26–7). The state is not hostile to Christianity, but is fickle. On the other hand, Christianity is not guilty of deliberate subversion, but poses a threat to the peace of the empire: Lysias sees Paul as a disturber of the peace (Acts 23:30).

Jervell's presentation is fuller than Franklin's. He argues that in the latter chapters of Acts we are seeing *Jewish* charges against Paul (21:21, 28; 23:29; 24:5; 25:8, 19; 28:17) rather than political charges initiated by the Roman authorities. Paul is being charged concerning his alleged teaching against Israel, the law and the temple. Charges of sedition come from the Jews (17:6–7; 24:5), whereas the Romans simply charge Paul with civil disturbance (16:20; 21:38; 25:8; cf. the charges against Jesus, Luke 23:2). Thus Luke's readers are Christian

---

[24] Ibid. 160.
[25] Jacob Jervell, *The Theology of the Acts of the Apostles*, 15–16, 86–8, 100–106, 134; Eric Franklin, *Christ the Lord*, 134–9.

Jews under pressure from their non-Christian compatriots. Jervell goes against the trend of scholarship in proposing that Luke is himself Jewish and wishes to show that Christian Jews are highly influential in the life of the early church.

Jervell observes that both Jews (Acts 2:23; 3:14–15; 4:10; 7:52; 10:39; 13:27–8) and Romans (Acts 4:27; 2:23; cf. 13:28) are responsible for the death of Jesus in Luke-Acts. Further, Luke's unflattering presentation of the Romans hardly allows Walaskay's approach. Thus Luke is showing his readers that the empire is no threat to the church: the empire cannot obstruct the progress of the gospel to the ends of the earth, even if it acts in concert with the Jewish authorities.[26] The church does not react politically towards the authorities: its only response is proclamation (Acts 4:20, 28–9; 5:29–32). Similarly, relations with the empire are through presenting the name of Jesus (Acts 9:15; 13:7; 24:14ff.; 26:1–32; Luke 12:11–12; 21:14–15); for now, Christianity is politically harmless, but when the kingdom of God appears the political powers will stand helpless (Luke 21:20–31).

In sum, in this view Luke has no 'theology of the state': he simply recognises its existence as a political reality, but he is clear that God is greater. Defiance of the empire only happens when it attempts to hinder the proclamation of the gospel.

Key Evidence

This survey of scholarship drives us back to the texts to see how far they support these views. I shall review the Romans' ways of administering their empire, focusing particularly on cities, the key contexts in Acts for Christian mission, and then reconsider seven features of Luke-Acts: the placing of Christianity in the context of the Roman empire; the location of Jesus within a Jewish frame-work; the trial of Jesus; the presentation of Roman officials and Roman justice; troubles caused by Paul; Jesus as Lord, king and saviour; and the ending of Acts. In each case I shall identify key passages and issues, and evaluate the relevance and strength of the evidence.

---

[26] Cf. Douglas R. Edwards, 'Surviving the Web of Roman Power', 179–201.

The administration of the Roman empire

This is a vast topic, and I shall of necessity concentrate on a small number of key points.[27] It is common in New Testament scholarship to assume that contacts between the Christians and the city authorities within the Roman empire can be taken as evidence of Christian relations with the empire. However, the Romans employed a system of delegated government, which meant that significant facets of city life were under the control of local people.

In New Testament times the empire was divided into provinces, some under direct imperial authority, others under senatorial control. In charge of each province was a governor, normally of senatorial rank, supported by a (usually very small) staff under his immediate control. Only in frontier or troublesome provinces, such as Judaea, were significant numbers of Roman troops present, in order to preserve Roman control and political stability. A key member of the governor's staff was the procurator, whose duties could include the collection of taxes, as well as looking after the emperor's interests.[28]

Within a province there would be a number of communities with 'city' (πόλις) status, and the nature of this status could vary considerably from one community to another.[29] Among its inhabitants, some were citizens of the city, and a smaller group (often much

---

[27] For (considerably) fuller accounts, see the following, to which my brief account is indebted: Joyce Reynolds, 'Cities', 15–51; Fergus Millar, *The Roman Empire and its Neighbours*, ch. 5; David W.J. Gill, 'The Roman Empire as a Context for the New Testament', 389–406; David W.J. Gill and Conrad H. Gempf (eds.), *The Book of Acts in its Graeco-Roman Setting*; Andrew Lintott, *Imperium Romanum*, esp. chs. 3–4, 8; A.H.M. Jones, *The Greek City from Alexander to Justinian*, esp. chs. iv, viii, xi; Anthony D. Macro, 'The Cities of Asia Minor under the Roman Imperium', 658–97. Valuable collections of source material in English translation are found in W.K. Lacey and B.W.J.G. Wilson, *Res Publica*, and Jo-Ann Shelton, *As the Romans Did*, esp. sections x, xii.

[28] Judaea and Egypt were exceptions to this structure in New Testament times, not having their own governor, but rather a procurator or prefect of equestrian rank: Emil Schürer, Geza Vermes and Fergus Millar, *The History of the Jewish People in the Age of Jesus Christ*, I:358.

[29] See Reynolds, 'Cities', 23, for a helpful taxonomy.

smaller) were Roman citizens. Philippi, Corinth and Pisidian Antioch were Roman colonies, all of whose citizens were Roman citizens – many were former soldiers granted citizenship on their retirement from the army.[30] Athens, by contrast, retained the feel of a Greek city with the Areopagus as its ruling council.[31] In this case, the Romans had taken an established Greek city and permitted its own civic structures to continue, but now overseen by the governor of the province of Achaia and his staff. As long as the city ran smoothly and peacefully, and Roman taxes were paid promptly, the governor would not be likely to interfere.

Typically a πόλις in the eastern empire would consist of an urban centre that controlled a surrounding territory, usually containing villages under the centre's jurisdiction – thus to think of a modern 'city' does not give quite the right picture. When the emperor granted the status of πόλις to an existing place he would allow the people to appoint (or, in the case of an established city, to continue to appoint) a council (βουλή) which could pass local laws, and to elect their own magistrates annually,[32] who dispensed justice in many matters and had their own subordinate officials.[33] Cities usually had a citizen assembly (ἐκκλησία), but under the Romans it was increasingly subject to the council, which tended to consist of members of the wealthy social élite.[34] Indeed, magistrates were frequently appointed from the council members, and were required to contribute financially to the city's affairs on appointment,[35] further limiting those who could be candidates for office.

---

[30] David W.J. Gill, 'Macedonia', 411–13.

[31] David W.J. Gill, 'Achaia', 441–3, 447.

[32] Luke gets the designation and jurisdiction of these officials right in place after place; see Colin J. Hemer and Conrad H. Gempf (ed.), *The Book of Acts in the Setting of Hellenistic History*, 115 (on 16:22), 119 (on 17:34), 121 (on 19:31), 122 (on 19:35), 123 (on 19:38), 153 with n. 152 (on 28:7).

[33] Cicero, *Epistulae ad Atticum* 6.1.15 (written c. 50 BC), says that he allowed Greeks to try cases between provincials under their own laws. Methods of election varied considerably across the empire: Reynolds, 'Cities', 26–7.

[34] Millar, *Roman Empire and its Neighbours*, 87.

[35] Reynolds, 'Cities', 36.

The powers of these local magistrates, councils and assemblies were circumscribed by those of the governor. Hence the Ephesian town clerk warns the citizens that the city is in danger of being charged with rioting (Acts 19:40), which could lead to the governor disbanding the citizen-assembly, punishing city officials or taking away privileges already granted to the city.[36]

More specifically, cases that could result in death or exile were reserved for the governor's judgement, as well as cases involving Roman citizens,[37] and some cases involving commercial questions or public order.[38] The governor would travel annually to various cities within his province to try such cases, and others that the local magistrates could not resolve.[39] In Achaia Luke records Gallio hearing the Jews' case against Paul in Corinth, the governor's seat (Acts 18:12–17).[40] In Judaea this comports well with John's assertion that the Jews were not allowed to 'put anyone to death' (John 18:31).[41]

It is within this setting that the Acts accounts of encounter between the Christians and the 'powers that be' should be seen. This limits the number of *direct* contacts between the Christians – and Paul in particular – and the Roman empire, as we shall see.

---

[36] Paul R. Trebilco, 'Asia', 344–5 (where examples are given).

[37] Macro, 'Cities of Asia Minor', 671. Hence the Philippian magistrates are taken aback when they realise they have beaten Roman citizens, thus acting in a case over which they have no jurisdiction (Acts 16:37–9).

[38] Bruce W. Winter, *Seek the Welfare of the City*, 107–8.

[39] See G.P. Burton, 'Proconsuls, Assizes and the Administration of Justice under the Empire', 92–106, for a careful description of the system of travelling assizes.

[40] Most governors had at least one legal advisor among their personal staff (cf. Acts 25:12), whereas Gallio, a noted jurist, gives his own judgement without consulting advisors.

[41] Supported by Josephus, *War* 2.117 = 2.8.1. See discussion (and further references) in George R. Beasley-Murray, *John* 308–10; D.A. Carson, *The Gospel according to John*, 590–2.

Christianity placed in the context of the Roman empire[42]

Luke alone among the canonical evangelists sets the coming of Jesus and the growth of the church in the context of the Roman empire. He identifies Augustus as emperor and Quirinius as governor of Syria when Jesus is born (Luke 2:1–2).[43] He offers a sixfold dating by Roman rulers for John beginning to preach (Luke 3:1–2). Throughout Luke-Acts readers who are aware of the ancient world are conscious that Paul, for example, is able to travel freely because of the benefits of Roman roads, harbours, ships and, above all, the *pax Romana*.[44] In Acts, particularly in the second half, Luke relates developments in the Christian community to the empire, referring to Roman officials from time to time and the interaction between the missionaries and these people.

However, this evidence is slight, for Luke never explicitly mentions the benefits of the *pax Romana* or the Roman road system.[45] If, as some urge,[46] this is a significant sign of Luke's positive view of the empire, he has not gone out of his way to draw attention to it. Paul's direct contacts with *Roman* officials are limited to Gallio in Corinth (18:12–17), the tribune in Jerusalem (21–2), Felix (23:31 – 24:26), Festus (24:27 – 26:32) and Julius the centurion (27:1, 11, 31, 43). The emperors themselves never appear in the narrative, but are always peripheral (e.g. Luke 2:1–2; 3:1–2; Acts 5:37; 11:28; 18:2).[47] Nero is not mentioned by name, although in places it must be him to whom a character refers (Acts 25:11–12, 21, 25–6).

---

[42] See Bond, *Pontius Pilate*, 140–1.

[43] The dating here is notoriously difficult; see discussion in John Nolland, *Luke 1–9:20*, 99–102 (particularly thorough); Joseph A. Fitzmyer, *Luke I–IX*, 400; Christopher F. Evans, *Saint Luke*, 193–5; I. Howard Marshall, *The Gospel of Luke*, 99–104; Raymond E. Brown, *The Birth of the Messiah*, 547–56.

[44] See Michael B. Thompson, 'The Holy Internet', 49–70; Michael Green, *Evangelism in the Early Church*, 14–16.

[45] On the latter, see David French, 'Acts and the Roman Roads of Asia Minor', 49–58.

[46] Walaskay, *And So We Came*, 25–7; Brown, *Birth of the Messiah*, 415–16.

[47] Robbins, 'Luke-Acts', 205–7.

Jesus acts within a Jewish 'religious' framework

For Conzelmann it is important that Luke places Jesus within a Jewish 'religious' framework,[48] for this proves that Luke is attempting to show Christianity as politically neutral and harmless. Luke, Conzelmann believes, is coming to terms with the delay of the parousia, and therefore is handling a situation where the church must come to a 'settlement' with the empire. Several lines of evidence are important to Conzelmann's case.

In Luke, John's preaching to the soldiers and tax-collectors (3:10ff.) includes the implicit instruction to be loyal to the state. John's arrest is for non-political reasons (3:19). Jesus' career is presented as non-political in the Nazareth scene (4:18ff.). When Herod seeks to 'see' Jesus it is because of his miracles, not for any political reason (9:7ff.; cf. 23:8). Jesus' death will be that of a prophet, not a political subversive (13:31ff.). At the entry to Jerusalem Jesus is acclaimed as 'king' in a non-political sense, for the goal of his journey is the temple (19:38). When the question of the political supremacy of Rome is raised explicitly, Jesus encourages submission to the emperor (20:20–6). Although the accusations against Jesus are framed politically (23:2), Luke makes it clear that the Jewish authorities are lying (20:20ff. shows that they themselves are disingenuous in their question; 23:18ff. shows that they are in fact in solidarity with political insurgents).

However, Conzelmann operates with a division of 'religion' and 'politics' untenable for the first century AD. To speak of Jesus in kingly terms was inevitably to speak politically, for that was the kind of king known in that world.[49] Further, to speak of Jesus as 'son of God' was to invoke a messianic, that is, a royal title (cf. Ps 2:7) with political overtones. To argue that Luke's insertion of 'king' into the triumphal entry is non-political is naïve in a world where Caesar was known as 'king'. For Jesus to read Isaiah 61:1ff. in the synagogue at Nazareth (4:16ff.) cannot be construed as apolitical, for it echoes jubilee legislation that presupposes Israel once again has control of

---

[48] Conzelmann, *Theology of St Luke*, 137–49.
[49] On this paragraph, see N.T. Wright, *Jesus and the Victory of God*, 2:97–8, 296–7, 310–11, 481–6; Marcus J. Borg, *Conflict, Holiness and Politics in the Teachings of Jesus*.

her own land.[50] For John to speak against Herod's marriage was to speak against the king's fitness to rule in a world where divine law concerning marriage was taken seriously.[51]

The question of tribute to Caesar (Luke 20:20–6) requires a little more discussion.[52] In a time and place where revolution was in the air Jesus' answer to the question whether tribute should be paid to Caesar would have been awaited with bated breath. If he said that tribute should be paid to Caesar, he would identify himself with the collaborators; if not, he would mark himself as a revolutionary and a danger to Rome. Jesus' brilliant answer, 'Give to Caesar that which is Caesar's, and to God that which is God's' (v. 25) avoids both horns of the dilemma. This answer echoes Mattathias's dying words, 'Pay back the Gentiles in full and obey the commands of the law' (ἀνταπόδοτε ἀνταπόδομα τοῖς ἔθνεᾶιν καὶ προσέχετε εἰς πρόσταγμα τοῦ νόμου, 1 Macc. 2:68). The first clause of Mattathias's words is unquestionably a revolutionary charter. Thus, facing someone holding a Roman coin with a blasphemous inscription,[53] Jesus' response was implicitly revolutionary, for it implied that Caesar should get what he deserved. Yet it was not explicitly so, for Jesus had not forbidden paying the census tax, and thereby avoided being arrested before he was ready. The second clause of Jesus' answer (in agreement with the second clause of

---

[50] Cf. Wright, *Jesus*, 294–5; Joel B. Green, *The Gospel of Luke*, 212–3; Nolland, *Luke 1–9:20*, 197; Sharon H. Ringe, *Jesus, Liberation, and the Biblical Jubilee*, 36–45; *contra* Robert C. Tannehill, *The Narrative Unity of Luke-Acts*, 1:67–8.

[51] Cf. Wright, *Jesus*, 160–2; Harold W. Hoehner, *Herod Antipas*, 142–4.

[52] What follows is based on Wright, *Jesus*, 502–7; cf. John Nolland, *Luke 18:35–24:53*, 955–61. For other views, see F.F. Bruce, 'Render to Caesar', 249–63, esp. 257–62; Marshall, *Luke*, 733–7; Joseph A. Fitzmyer, *Luke X–XXIV*, 1284–98; J. Duncan M. Derrett, 'Luke's Perspective on Tribute to Caesar', 38–48, esp. 41–3.

[53] H. StJ. Hart, 'The Coin of "Render unto Caesar …" (A Note on Some Aspects of Mark 12:13–17; Matt. 22:15–22; Luke 20:20–26)', 241–8, shows that the inscription would probably be TI(BERIUS) CAESAR DIVI AUG(USTI) F(ILIUS) AUGUSTUS: PONTIFEX MAXIMUS (= 'Tiberius Caesar, son of the divine Augustus, Augustus: high priest') – thus making blasphemous claims alongside the offensive presence of Caesar's εἰκών (image).

Mattathias's words) echoes Israel's call to worship the one true God (e.g. Ps. 96:7–10; Deut. 6:4–5) and to avoid idolatry. Thus, faced with this blasphemous Roman coin, Jesus implicitly states that possession of it involves compromise with paganism – and therefore gives a clarion call to faithfulness to Yahweh by calling his hearers to follow Jesus' way of the kingdom. Jesus' two-edged answer could be accused of many things, but that it was 'political', in both Jewish and Roman contexts, is hard to deny.

The trial of Jesus

It is clearly crucial to understanding Luke's view of the empire to consider the empire's treatment of Jesus. Pilate as Roman governor three times declares Jesus innocent of any crime (Luke 23:4, 14, 22) and invokes the client-king Herod as having come to the same conclusion (Luke 23:15). Herod himself has failed to gain any answer from Jesus after having earlier sought to see him and, reportedly, plotted to kill him (Luke 23:8–11; cf. 9:7–9; 13:31–2). The centurion at the foot of the cross likewise declares Jesus to be innocent (Luke 23:47; contrast Mark 15:33; Matt. 27:54). So who is responsible for the death of Jesus from Luke's perspective?

A key passage for understanding Luke's view is Acts 4:27–30, which asserts that opposition to Jesus is the factor uniting Pilate, Herod, the Gentiles and the 'peoples of Israel'.[54] To assert, as some do,[55] that the Jewish people alone are held responsible for the death of Jesus is to overstate the case. Luke's presentation is more nuanced, for he locates responsibility on the Jewish side with the Jewish leaders in Jerusalem and, to a lesser degree, the people of Jerusalem.[56] This is clear, not least, since it is only in Jerusalem itself that the apostles speak of 'you' as responsible for killing Jesus (Acts 2:36; 3:13, 14, 17; 4:10; 5:30; 7:52; cf. 5:28). Further, on the one occasion outside Jerusalem where Paul speaks of responsibility for the death of Jesus, he attributes it to the Jerusalem residents and especially their leaders (Acts 13:26–7).

---

[54] Jervell, *Theology of Acts*, 100–101.
[55] Especially Sanders, *Jews in Luke-Acts*.
[56] Weatherly, *Jewish Responsibility*, esp. ch. 2.

It is also clear from Luke's characterisation of Pilate that the Roman system is by no means guiltless in this regard.[57] Luke 18:31–4 asserts that Jesus will be handed over to the Gentiles (v. 32). Pilate is named in speeches in Acts concerning the death of Jesus (Acts 3:13; 4:27; 13:28). In the Lukan passion narrative, while Pilate pronounces Jesus innocent three times, he nevertheless gives him over to be executed (Luke 23:25). This portrays Pilate as all the more culpable, not least because the verb παραδίδωμι (give over) is used on at least twenty occasions by Luke as indicating 'giving over' in persecution, arrest, betrayal or execution, especially in the passion narrative, where it is the only sense in which this verb is used.[58]

Certainly Luke regards the purposes of God as being achieved through the death of Jesus (not least in Acts 4:28), but this does not exonerate either the Jewish or Roman authorities. Both share the blame, just as both Jews and Gentiles may benefit from the fruits of the death of Jesus, as Acts makes clear by the response among both to the preaching of the gospel.

The presentation of Roman officials and Roman justice

This is a significant group of evidence on our question, for there are several occasions when the empire's officials, soldiers or justice system impinge on Luke-Acts, especially Acts. We may divide the passages into those that present positive and negative views of the empire.

As far as positive aspects go, six features of Luke's *Dopplewerk* come to mind. First, John the baptiser's preaching to tax-collectors and soldiers (Luke 3:1–10) avoids telling them to withdraw from their occupations, but rather instructs them on how to conduct their vocations in a manner consistent with being baptised by John. Given that these people are in both cases likely to be Jewish[59] (for

---

[57]   See Bond, *Pontius Pilate*, 150–60.

[58]   Luke 9:44; 12:58; 18:32; 20:20; 21:12, 16; 22:4, 6, 21, 22, 48; 23:25; 24:7, 20; Acts 3:13; 8:3; 12:4; 21:11; 22:4; 27:1; see Weatherly, *Jewish Responsibility*, 96 (the list of references is an expanded version of his). The verb is used thirty times in total in Luke-Acts.

[59]   With Marshall, *Luke*, 143; Nolland, *Luke 1–9:20*, 150; Fitzmyer, *Luke I–IX*, 470; Evans, *Saint Luke*, 241; *contra* Walaskay, *And So We Came*, 31 (with 81, n. 82); Green, *Luke*, 180.

John's was a Jewish renewal movement), these instructions are at least supportive of the empire, since they are compatible with Augustan ideals for these groups.[60]

Second, Walaskay regards Luke 22:24–7 as an edited version of Mark 10:42–5, and in particular proposes that the replacement of the compound verbs κατακυριεύω and κατεξουσιάζω (Mark 10:42; they imply domineering rule) by the simple forms κυριεύω and ἐξουσιάζω (Luke 22:25; they do not carry 'domineering' overtones) suggests that Luke is 'toning down' Mark's wording to sound less anti-empire. However, it is unlikely that the Lukan passage is a true parallel to the Markan,[61] for the verbal agreement is poor: of sixty-seven words in Luke 22:24–7, only sixteen occur in the same form in Mark – including four definite articles, four conjunctions, three third-person plural nouns, and the phrases οὐχ οὕτως and ἐν ὑμῖν. No verbal forms are common to the two passages, and the only noun they share is ἐθνῶν. Further, Luke rarely relocates material from its Markan sequence, but rather uses the material in the same order. Jeremias points to only two small deviations before the passion narrative (Luke 6:17–19; 8:19–21) and concludes that deviations imply that Luke is not using Mark.[62] In sum, it is unlikely that we should draw any conclusions from this proposed parallel, since it is not a real parallel. We may add that, from the perspective of Luke's first readers, such subtleties would be likely to be invisible, for they probably did not have access to Mark's Gospel (nor, indeed, a Gospels Synopsis!).[63]

---

[60] Walaskay, *And So We Came*, 29–32.

[61] For this paragraph (including fuller detail on differences between Mark and Luke), see Steve Walton, *Leadership and Lifestyle*, 110–15, and Peter K. Nelson, *Leadership and Discipleship*, 124–31, in agreement with Marion L. Soards, *The Passion according to Luke*, 30–1; Sydney H.T. Page, 'The Authenticity of the Ransom Logion (Mark 10:45b)', 148–54; Joel B. Green, *The Death of Jesus*, 44–6; Vincent Taylor, *The Passion Narrative of St Luke*, 61–4; Nolland, *Luke 18:35–24:53*, 1062–3.

[62] Joachim Jeremias, *The Eucharistic Words of Jesus*, 98.

[63] Cf. C.K. Barrett, *A Critical and Exegetical Commentary on the Acts of the Apostles*, II:1: 'We cannot suppose that Luke wrote his gospel with the notion that it should be published in one of four parallel columns in a Synopsis.'

Third, the lack of any reporting of Roman persecution of the early Christian community in Jerusalem suggests that the Jesus movement was not seen as a political threat, for the Romans could and did round up and execute the followers of would-be revolutionaries.[64]

Fourth, Luke presents Roman officials and (especially) centurions positively, drawing attention to their godliness or justice. The centurion of Capernaum (Luke 7:1–10; cf. Matthew 8:5–13) is presented more fulsomely by Luke than by Matthew, for Luke includes a speech telling Jesus of the man's piety (7:4–5). The portrait of Cornelius (Acts 10:1 – 11:18) echoes this centurion's godliness, for Cornelius is 'devout and God-fearing', he gives to the needy, prays (10:2) and is commended by the angel (10:4). When Peter hears about Cornelius, these qualities are underlined (10:22). In addition, some Roman officials – such as the proconsul in Cyprus, Sergius Paulus (Acts 13:7, 12) – believe.[65]

Fifth, Paul is portrayed as submitting to the legal process, and generally being helpful to Roman officials. He does not resist arrest; he answers the charges against him and speaks respectfully to the courts (e.g. Acts 24:10; 26:2–3); he assists and advises Julius the centurion during the voyage to Rome (27:21–6, 30–2, 33–6). However, Paul is no doormat, for on key occasions he expects justice and exercises his privileges as a Roman citizen (22:25–9; 25:11[66]). Similarly, he speaks frankly with Felix about judgement to come (24:25).

Sixth, Paul is regularly found innocent and/or treated well by Roman officials irrespective of their acceptance of the Christian faith. In Corinth the proconsul Gallio finds that he has no case to answer (Acts 18:14–15). Claudius Lysias, the commander of the Jerusalem garrison, saves Paul from the mob (21:31–4), permits him

---

[64] E.g. Josephus, *War* 2.261–3 = 2.13.5 (the Egyptian false prophet); *Antiquities* 20.102 = 2.5.2 (the sons of Judas the Galilean); *War* 2.118 = 2.8.1; *Antiquities* 18.4–10 = 18.1.1 (Judas the Galilean); *Antiquities* 20.97–8 = 20.5.1 and Acts 5:36–7 (Theudas).

[65] The tax-collector Zacchaeus (Luke 19:1–10) and the Philippian jailer (Acts 16:27–34) are not *Roman* officials, but local officials, even though Zacchaeus would have been seen as a Roman collaborator by the Jewish people at large.

[66] Cf. Paul's response to the local magistrates in the Roman colony of Philippi (Acts 16:35–9).

to speak to the crowd (21:37–40a), complies with Paul's request to exercise the privileges of his Roman citizenship (22:24–9), protects Paul from the Sanhedrin (23:10), and finally sends Paul to Caesarea, away from the plot to kill him, accompanied by a letter expressing the view that Paul has no charge to answer (23:16–30). Felix appears to regard Paul as innocent and only keeps him in prison from expediency (24:23, 27). Festus judges that Paul is innocent of crime (25:25), a verdict confirmed by the client-king Herod Agrippa II (26:32). Julius treats Paul well by allowing him to visit his friends in Sidon (27:3) and by protecting him when the soldiers plan to kill all the prisoners during the shipwreck (27:42–3). Publius, the first man of Malta,[67] welcomes Paul and his companions and treats them well (28:7).

We may also observe that the charges against Paul are almost always presented as an internal Jewish argument in which Roman officials do not wish to become involved (Acts 18:13–15; 23:27–9; 25:19; cf. 26:2–3).[68] The magistrates are only concerned to keep public order, and do not wish to become involved in 'theology'.

Such are the positive aspects of Christianity in relation to the Roman empire. Two striking negative aspects of the portrait of the Jesus movement in relation to the empire should also be noted.

First, Luke underlines the fact that Jerusalem will fall to the Romans, and highlights this more than Mark or Matthew (Luke 21; Mark 13; Matthew 24), particularly Luke 21:20 (which makes it clear that Jerusalem is being spoken about) and 21:24 (which speaks of Jerusalem being trampled by the Gentiles).

Second, Luke presents Roman officialdom 'warts and all', and does not hesitate to tell of failings and corruption.[69] Pilate is represented as weak and swayed by the Jewish leaders into acting

---

[67] Publius may be either a Roman official or a local official whose jurisdiction was recognised by the Romans, after the manner of city magistrates; see discussion in Barrett, *Acts*, II:1224–5; Witherington, *Acts*, 779.

[68] Jervell, *Theology of Acts*, 87–8, astutely observes that the charges against Paul are as a false teacher of Israel (Acts 21:21, 28; 25:8; 24:5–6; 23:29; cf. 25:19). In the Roman colony of Philippi (Acts 16:20–1) the issue is ironically to do with Paul's Jewishness.

[69] Ibid. 103–4; Witherington, *Acts*, 811; Brian M. Rapske, *The Book of Acts and Paul in Roman Custody*, 431; Franklin, *Christ the Lord*, 136–9; Bond, *Pontius Pilate*, 142–3.

unjustly, knowing Jesus to be innocent (Luke 23:3, 14, 22, 24).[70] The verb ἐπικρίνω (v. 24) is used elsewhere in judicial contexts,[71] which suggests that Pilate is here giving a formal judgement in his own person, and thus his conduct is not excused by Luke. This adds to the description of Pilate's act of killing the Galileans (Luke 13:1), which Luke alone reports. We may grant that the focus of Luke 13:1ff. is not on Pilate's conduct, but on God's judgement on those who reject his messengers,[72] but nevertheless Luke does report this unflattering action (which appears not untypical of the historical Pilate[73]).

Similarly, when Paul travels, Roman officials fail to offer him protection or justice in cities under direct Roman law (as opposed to Hellenistic cities), whether in Pisidian Antioch (Acts 13:50–1),[74] Lystra (14:19), Philippi (16:20–4, 35–9).[75] The primary concern of the officials is to get the problem (Paul) to go away, rather than with the truth of the matter or the requirements of justice. Similarly, a careful reading suggests that the Roman proconsul Gallio disregards the accusations against Paul, not because they are untrue, but because of his apparent disdain for Paul's accusers: his address ὦ Ἰουδαῖοι (18:14), in combination with the feeling of exasperation conveyed in the rest of his ruling (18:14–15) and the fact that Gallio 'drove' (ἀπήλασεν, 18:16) the accusers from before the judgement seat, all suggest bias by Gallio against Paul's accusers.[76] If the 'all' who assault Sosthenes (18:17) are (Gentile) bystanders, this suggests anti-Semitic feeling, more widely than Gallio's views, was present in Corinth.[77]

---

[70] 'In the governor's court, injustice has triumphed over justice' (Bond, *Pontius Pilate*, 159).

[71] E.g. Plato, *Laws* 6.768a; Aristophanes, *Wasps* 1434; Josephus *War* 6.416 = 6.9.1; *Antiquities* 14.192 = 14.10.2; cf. Bond, *Pontius Pilate*, 156.

[72] Walaskay, *And So We Came*, 24.

[73] N.T. Wright, *The New Testament and the People of God*, 173–4.

[74] See G.H.R. Horsley, *New Documents Illustrating Early Christianity*, vol. 3:30, proposing that the 'leading men' (Acts 13:50) are Roman magistrates.

[75] Both Lystra and Philippi were Roman colonies, where one might expect some protection for Roman citizens, as happens eventually in Philippi.

[76] Cassidy, *Society and Politics in Acts*, 92.

[77] So Bruce, *Book of Acts*, 353–4; Ernst Haenchen, *The Acts of the Apostles*, 536–7; Luke T. Johnson, *The Acts of the Apostles*, 329; Witherington,

When it comes to Paul's trials in Jerusalem and Caesarea, although Paul is protected by Roman officials from the attempts of the Jewish authorities to do away with him, the tribune Claudius Lysias transfers Paul to Caesarea despite believing him to be innocent of crime (Acts 23:27), Felix hopes for a bribe and keeps Paul in custody to please the Jews (24:26–7), and Festus is (understandably, as a new governor) more concerned with pleasing the Jews than giving Paul justice (25:9, 25). Ultimately, Paul appeals to Caesar because he does not expect to receive justice from Festus (25:11) – and with good reason! The result of the actions (or non-actions) of Felix and Festus is that Paul unnecessarily spends four years imprisoned. If, as some emphasise,[78] Roman officials recognise Paul's innocence, his continuing imprisonment suggests that Roman justice is corrupt – hardly a persuasive argument if Luke is seeking to persuade the church to trust the state, or if Luke hopes to convince Roman officials that they have nothing to fear from the church.

Luke offers a mixed (and, therefore, probably realistic) portrait of the Roman officials who encounter Jesus and Paul.[79] Such a portrait would offer to Christians in various situations in the ancient world models of handling relationships with the authorities.[80]

Trouble caused by Paul

On several key occasions Paul is presented as the source of trouble in the cities he visits. In places this is the result of Jewish agitators persuading the populace to attack Paul, such as Antioch (Acts 13:50), Iconium (14:2, 4–5), Lystra (14:19), Thessalonica (17:5–8), Beroea (17:13), Corinth (18:12–13), and Jerusalem (21:27–30). But on other

---

[77] *(continued)* *Acts* 554–5; contra Joseph A. Fitzmyer, *The Acts of the Apostles*, 630–1. Barrett, *Acts*, II:875–6, adopts a mediating position in which Jews and Greeks combined to attack Sosthenes.

[78] E.g. Wengst, *Pax Romana*, 98–9.

[79] Rapske, *Paul in Roman Custody*, 190–1.

[80] Ibid. 190, helpfully suggests that Paul's appeal to his Roman citizenship at times would demonstrate that Christian faith did not forbid use of this privilege in order to receive better treatment, while the wider example of Paul would also suggest that the use of such privileges should never be a way of avoiding suffering for the sake of the gospel.

occasions it is Gentiles opposed to Jewish practices (Philippi, 16:20–1) or Gentile traders who are being harmed economically by Paul's ministry (Ephesus, 19:23–8). Neither group of events would persuade Roman officials reading Acts that Christians were politically harmless or neutral and that all the trouble was the work of Jewish agitators – Paul is simply a cause of trouble wherever he goes, and the charges of civil disturbance brought against him (16:20; 21:38; 25:8) would reinforce this view. For Christian readers these stories would highlight the vulnerability of proclaiming the gospel in the face of hostile opponents, whether Jewish, Hellenistic or Roman.

Jesus as Lord, king and saviour

Luke stresses that Jesus is 'Lord', for he uses this title for Jesus very frequently,[81] especially after the resurrection (but also – and program-matically – in the birth narratives, Luke 2:11), to the extent that we may see this as Luke's standard way of describing Jesus' present position. Luke never mentions Caesar's claim to be lord,[82] but to use κύριος so prominently for Jesus could not but remind readers living in the empire of this claim and would suggest that Luke was making a counter-claim for Jesus over against Caesar (as indeed he was).

Similarly, Jesus is referred to as 'king' by Luke more frequently than the other evangelists,[83] not least in the birth narratives in

---

[81] Κύριος is the most frequent title for Jesus in Acts, found some sixty times: see James D.G. Dunn, 'ΚΥΡΙΟΣ in Acts', 241–53; D.L. Jones, 'The Title ΚΥΡΙΟΣ in Acts', 85–101; Steve Walton, 'Where Does the Beginning of Acts End?', 460.

[82] See Adolf Deissmann, *Light from the Ancient East*, 353–5; Tajra, *Trial of St Paul*, 36, the latter observing that κύριος was used in poetry of the emperor as early as Augustan times.

[83] Βασιλεύς and βασιλεύω are used seven times of Jesus by Luke (cf. Mat-thew six times; Mark six times – in both cases mainly in the passion narra-tive): Luke 1:32–3; 19:38 (here Walaskay, *And So We Came*, 17, correctly argues that Conzelmann, *Theology of St Luke*, 139, is mistaken in arguing that Luke's introduction of βασιλεύς into Mark's story preserves a non-political view of kingship); 22:29–30; 23:2, 37–8; Acts 17:7. Brent Kinman, *Jesus' Entry into Jerusalem in the Context of Lukan Theology and the Politics of His Day*, esp. 91–103, demonstrates that Luke heightens the sense

reference to him 'reigning' (Luke 1:33) and the insertion of 'king' into the acclamation at the 'triumphal entry' (Luke 19:38). The charge against Jesus, which he does not deny, is that he claims to be a king (Luke 23:2; cf. 23:37–8). Behind the claim that the Christians proclaim 'another king' (Acts 17:7) surely stands Caesar's claim to be king.

Luke also uses the language of 'salvation' more frequently than the other evangelists,[84] to the extent that it can be claimed as the main theme of Luke-Acts,[85] and specifically calls Jesus σωτήρ (Luke 2:11; Acts 5:31; 13:23). Again, this echoes language used of Caesar.[86]

The use of these three groups of words so prominently for Jesus suggests that Luke presents the early Christians as subversively using Caesar's titles for Jesus. When we add to this the strong statements in the face of the Jewish authorities that obeying God is more important than obeying mere human beings (Acts 4:19; 5:29), the reading of Jesus' 'render to Caesar' saying proposed above, and Luke's view that the kingdoms of the world are in the hands of the

---

[83] (*continued*) of Jesus' kingship in his account of the entry into Jerusalem. Walaskay, *And So We Came*, 22, notes that Luke 1:52; 4:18–19; 12:49, 51; Acts 5:29, 42; 21:38; 28:31 imply an anti-Caesar stance. In conversation, Dr Gerald Borchert proposed to me that John makes the *theme* of the kingship of Jesus prominent, particularly from John 12 onwards, even though John does not use the *language* of kingship as frequently as Luke; Dr Borchert will argue this in his forthcoming second volume on John (NAC).

[84] Twenty-five times in Luke; twenty-two times in Acts (Matthew fifteen times; Mark sixteen times, John eight times). Luke programmatically signals this theme in his birth narrative by using the word group six times (1:47, 69, 71, 77; 2:11, 30), as well as summarising the Christian message using τοῦτο τὸ σωτήριον τοῦ θεοῦ at the end of Acts (28:28), thus forming an *inclusio*.

[85] I. Howard Marshall, *Luke: Historian*, esp. 94–102.

[86] E.g. Julius Caesar is described as 'the god made manifest ... and common saviour of human life' (*SIG*[3] §760; trans. from Deissmann, *Light*, 344); Augustus is one 'providence ... [sent] us and those after us a saviour who put an end to war and established all things' (*IGRR* III §719; trans. from Naphtali Lewis and Meyer Reinhold (eds.), *Roman Civilization*, 2:64, and 'saviour of the entire world' (*OGIS* II §458; my trans.); and Claudius is 'saviour of the world' (*IGRR* IV §12; Oakes's trans.) and 'god who is saviour and benefactor' (*IGRR* IV §584; Oakes's trans.). See further Peter Oakes, *Philippians*, ch. 5 (Dr Oakes kindly allowed me to see a draft that outlines these references).

devil (Luke 4:5–6[87]), we have a picture of a movement that, to a Roman loyalist, could not but be seen as subversive and anti-emperor.

The ending of Acts

Acts ends with Paul living in his own rented accommodation able to preach the gospel unhindered (ἀκωλύτως,[88] 28:31), and without his hearing before Caesar having taken place. The question why Luke ends at this point has long been debated, but we shall consider only its contribution to our understanding of Luke's view of the Roman empire.

Cassidy argues that this ending provides completeness: Paul's faithful testimony before Caesar is complete 'in principle'.[89] As Acts closes, Paul is close to appearing before the emperor's tribunal in Rome and we know from assurances given by God that he will appear there (23:11; 27:23–4). Further, throughout Paul has spoken faithfully for Jesus, so we may be confident that he will do so before Caesar. Luke goes on to present a scene in Rome where Paul speaks in precisely that manner (28:17–20, 23, 25–8).

All this is true enough, but hardly answers our question about Luke's view of the empire. As far as the fate of Paul is concerned, the ending of Acts is unresolved.[90] If Luke had reported Paul's execution[91] this would have told against any presentation of the empire as acting justly (although we have seen reasons to doubt this as a uniform picture throughout Luke-Acts). If Paul had been acquitted, then the story would have been complete from the perspective of Paul's political innocence being demonstrated – and thus the political harmlessness of Christianity would be clear.

---

[87] Jervell, *Theology of Acts*, 106; Evans, *Saint Luke*, 259; Green, *Luke*, 194.

[88] A legal term: MM, 20; BDAG, 40; Tajra, *Trial of St Paul*, 192–3; Barrett, *Acts*, II:1253.

[89] Cassidy, *Society and Politics in Acts*, 167–70.

[90] Franklin, *Christ the Lord*, 134–6.

[91] Reported by Eusebius, *Historia ecclesiastica* 2.25, and hinted at in 1 Clem. 5.1–6.1. For discussion see F.F. Bruce, *Paul*, 441–55; E.P. Sanders, *Paul*, 16–17; Jerome Murphy-O'Connor, OP, *Paul*, 368–81.

Some[92] suggest that the hints of martyrdom during the book (Acts 20:25, 29, 37–8;[93] 21:11–14; 28:17–20) show that Luke and his readers already knew that Paul had been executed in Rome, and so that part of the story did not need telling. Indeed, had Luke told it, it would have distracted from the point he wished to make.[94] On this view, Luke's concern is not with whether Paul is acquitted or condemned, but simply with his being in Rome at all – but it would hardly encourage a positive view of the empire.

It is not easy to decide the date at which Luke wrote. If it was before the trial of Paul, then Paul's fate was unresolved at that point, which would explain why Luke did not report the result.[95] If Luke wrote after the death of Paul (whether or not Paul was initially released before being imprisoned again before his execution), he must have had good reason for not including this event. Perhaps the explanation, whatever Luke's date of writing, is in his demonstration that Paul was able to preach about Jesus freely for two years in the heart of the empire (28:30–1). If Paul could do this, then he – and, by extension, the Christian community – was regarded by the empire as innocent of crime.[96] Acts 28:31 closes with the portrait of the word of God unhindered, triumphant over human attempts to imprison its messengers, and that would speak powerfully to Luke's Christian readers in their attempts to be faithful to God in their day.[97]

Evaluation of Theories

In considering the theories outlined at the beginning of this chapter, our chief concerns must be how far each manages to get

---

[92] E.g. R.P.C. Hanson, *The Acts*, 31, 203–4; Haenchen, *Acts*, 731–2.

[93] For discussion of the Acts 20 verses, which leave Paul's fate open, rather than certainly speaking of his death, see Walton, *Leadership and Lifestyle*, 78–80.

[94] Although Acts 7:54–60; 12:1–2 show that Luke does not shy away from reporting the death of faithful believers.

[95] Although 28:30 implies that *something* happened to bring the two-year period to an end (Witherington, *Acts*, 807).

[96] Bruce, *Book of Acts*, 511; Haenchen, *Acts*, 726; Rapske, *Paul in Roman Custody*, 191.

[97] Cf. Fitzmyer, *Acts*, 797, and numerous others.

the variety of data from Luke-Acts into view, and how much explanatory power the theory has for Luke's intentions in writing.

Luke's readership has been widely debated, and is beyond the scope of this chapter. I simply re-emphasise that we should be cautious in mirror-reading Luke-Acts for its audience, particularly in seeking to find a section of Luke's readership for every individual emphasis of the two volumes (see above, pp. 8–9). Luke may have had reasons other than his audience's needs for recording an event – such as that it happened and was important for the church as part of its historical foundation.

To turn, then, to the different proposals, we must declare the claim that Luke is not interested in politics as barren. There is too much politically sensitive material for this view to be tenable when Luke-Acts is read in its first-century settings, both Jewish and Graeco-Roman. Nevertheless, Jervell identifies a crucial point, which is that Luke's *central* concern is not political; rather, Luke focuses on what God is doing, and other topics arise in relation to God's actions.[98] We shall return to this below.

We must regard the 'political apology' view as inadequate, for it omits too much important data, as I have repeatedly indicated. The greatest difficulty of this view is that, if one of Luke's primary purposes was to persuade Roman officials of the harmlessness of Christianity, he has been far too subtle to succeed and has included far too much extraneous material. More than that, his presentation of Roman officials is far from flattering, particularly his portrayal of Pilate's involvement in the death of Jesus. The fact that Paul is regularly a cause of civil unrest in cities he visits would not commend Christianity to Roman officials charged with main-taining the *pax Romana* – indeed, Acts ends without any verdict on Paul's case. Nor would the presence of a Zealot among Jesus' disciples add to these officials' sense of security. Moreover, the

---

[98] It is noticeable that θεός is the commonest verbal subject in Acts (sixty-three times in the singular); note esp. Acts 11:17–18; 14:27; 15:4, 7–8, 12, 14; 16:10; 21:19. The Lukan themes of fulfilment and God's plan are both suggestive for this point also; see David Peterson, 'The Motif of Fulfilment and the Purpose of Luke-Acts', 83–104; John T. Squires, *The Plan of God in Luke-Acts*; John T. Squires, 'The Plan of God in the Acts of the Apostles', 19–39.

claims that Jesus was 'another king' (Acts 17:7), 'lord' and 'saviour' made repeatedly in Luke-Acts would clash with Caesar's claims to these titles.

A subsidiary part of this view is often that Luke is presenting Christianity as a subspecies of Judaism; in view of the distance Luke at times places between Jews who believe the gospel and those who oppose it, we may nuance this point to say that it is likely that Luke is presenting Christianity as the true Judaism. In common with Paul, Matthew and John (at least), Luke sees no future for a Judaism that rejects its Messiah, Jesus.

The 'ecclesial apology' view, which sees Luke-Acts as commending collaboration with the empire as the way forward, fails to account for material critical of the empire. Luke-Acts contains much that would damage the estimation of the empire in Christian eyes, including Pilate's share in the death of Jesus and the continuing detention of Paul for four years, even though he was successively adjudged to be innocent by the Roman officials Claudius Lysias, Felix and Festus. Further, we lack evidence that there were Christians acting provocatively towards the empire or awaiting its apocalyptic collapse, apart from the doubtful inferences drawn from Luke-Acts by Maddox and Walaskay.[99]

Esler's 'legitimation' view is more nuanced and, at significant points close to the truth. Luke *is* writing to offer assurance to his readers in their faith (Luke 1:3–4[100]). Whether that readership includes those outside, or on the fringe of the church is debatable, but that it includes those inside the church is surely clear. However, we may doubt the likelihood of Esler's scenario, that Luke's congregation included a significant group of Romans for whom Luke is seeking to legitimate Christian faith, in particular to demonstrate to them the compatibility of Christian faith with allegiance to the empire. First (See above, pp. 8–9), Esler's mirror-reading of Luke-Acts is at best speculative. Second, the presence of

---

[99] Esler, *Community and Gospel in Luke-Acts*, 209. Esler observes this blind spot in Walaskay and Maddox, but apparently does not realise that he argues in the same manner in claiming that the presence of Roman officials presented positively in Luke-Acts implies that Luke's church contained such people.

[100] See Loveday Alexander, *The Preface to Luke's Gospel*, esp. 136–42.

significant materials that stress the *in*compatibility of Christian faith
with the 'metanarrative' claims of Caesar to supremacy suggests that
Luke's view is not as straightforward as this: Luke's Jesus is Lord,
king and saviour – all imperial titles – and his followers 'must
obey[101] God rather than any human authority' (Acts 5:29; cf.
4:19–20).

Cassidy's 'allegiance-conduct-witness' proposal represents a further
level of nuancing and manages to fit more of the data in. His proposal
that Luke writes to affirm and support his readers in their Christian
faith by sharing his own faith agrees substantially with Esler's view
and is likely to be correct, providing we understand it in the sense of
assuring his readers of the *truth* of that which he writes (Luke 1:3–4),
rather than simply sharing his own story (as we might say).

Given that Luke has such a concern for mission and witness – for
God's action to spread the gospel is one of the major themes of Acts
beginning, programmatically, in 1:8[102] – it is likely that he writes in
part to encourage the church of his day to preserve or recover a
readiness to witness faithfully and to take risks in mission at God's
prompting. It is also likely that Luke realises that some of this
testimony will be given under adversity, not least because he records
Jesus as predicting this and the earliest Christians as fulfilling it
(e.g. Luke 12:4–12; Acts 20:19, 23–5, 28–31[103]). Cassidy is also
correct in observing the high proportion of Luke's narrative given
over to Paul's testimony before Roman officials.

Nevertheless, Cassidy finds it hard to handle the preponderance of
passages where Roman officials are presented kindly, even warmly, as
fair, efficient and helpful to Paul. As we have seen, Luke chooses to
present these people positively in significant cases, which suggests
that he is not only seeking to help Christians facing pressure from the
authorities, but also those dealing with friendlier versions of the
'powers that be'. The ending of Acts, which presents Paul preaching

---

[101] Πειθαρχεῖν, a word that can connote political obedience; e.g.
Aristotle, *Politics* 1262b3; Herodotus, *Histories* 5.91.1 (LSJ, 1353).

[102] Haenchen, *Acts*, 144, rightly observes, 'As Acts presents it, the Christian
Church is a *missionary* Church' (italics his). Note the summaries at Acts 2:47;
5:42; 6:7; 9:31, 42; 12:24; 16:5; 18:11; 19:10, 20; 28:30–1, each identifying
the growth of the church (or the word) as the focus of what God is doing.

[103] See discussion in Walton, *Leadership and Lifestyle*, 87–9, 122–4.

'unhindered' (20:31) in Rome, suggests a more positive view of the empire's treatment of Christians than Cassidy leads us to expect. While Luke is by no means uncritically pro-Roman, he certainly does not portray the empire in similar vein to Revelation, as the beast rising from the sea to oppose the people of God (Rev. 13). Rather, he sees the empire as a system through which God can and does work.[104]

This leads to a key criticism of Cassidy, which is that he seems to subsume all of Luke-Acts under the heading of political and social issues.[105] Against this, we need to assert that Luke's primary concern is with what *God* is doing by the Spirit and through the Christian community.[106] Luke-Acts is focused on the progress of the word of God around the Mediterranean basin and, in this context, Luke is concerned with who God is (and thus Christology and pneumatology are central to his theology) and how to respond to God as he has now revealed himself in the life, ministry, death and resurrection of Jesus, the Messiah. How, then, might we summarise Luke's view of the empire in this context?

Proposal

We may summarise the view of Luke's presentation of the Roman empire by a series of affirmations.

First, Luke writes purposively when he writes about the Roman empire, and not merely descriptively. He tells his stories of Christians, and particularly Paul, relating to the empire to help his readers see what shape Christian discipleship in relation to the empire might take in their day. The prologue to the Gospel suggests this strongly (Luke 1:3–4).

Second, Luke offers a variety of perspectives on Christian relations with the empire. When the empire is friendly and acting justly, Christians can expect the state to allow them freedom to bear

---

[104] Cf. John M.G. Barclay, review of Richard J. Cassidy, *Society and Politics in the Acts of the Apostles*, 577.

[105] Cf. Robert F. O'Toole, SJ, review of Richard J. Cassidy, *Society and Politics in the Acts of the Apostles*, 427.

[106] See n. 98. I shall argue this *in extenso* in a commentary on Acts now in progress.

witness to Jesus and to speak 'unhindered'. For this situation, models include the eighteen-month period in Corinth either side of the hearing before Gallio (18:1–18a), the two years or more in Ephesus of (relatively) peaceful ministry (19:1–22) and the visit to Malta (28:1–10) – to say nothing of the closing scene in Rome (28:30–1). Luke's presentation of the innocence of Paul and Jesus of the charges against them would encourage Christians to live at peace with the authorities as far as it lay with them to do so. When the empire behaves thus towards Christians, Robbins's view that the relationship of church and Caesar is symbiotic has much to commend it, as does his claim that in such situations Christians work by negotiation with the Roman authorities.

But Luke does not have a romantic, idealised view of the empire. He is well aware that Christians can be harassed, persecuted and arrested for their witness to Jesus, both officially and unofficially. In such situations the examples of Jesus, Peter and John, Stephen, James the brother of Jesus, and Paul offer pictures of faithfully maintaining the 'good confession' (cf. 1 Tim. 6:12–14), in some cases leading to deliverance, and in others to punishment or even death.[107] The repeated emphasis on the innocence of the Christians and of Jesus shows that Luke's readers should not fight with the enemy's weapons, whether violence or falsehood, but rather that they should offer testimony to Jesus in similar manner to Peter and John, Stephen or Paul, relying on Jesus' promise that the Spirit will show them how to speak (Luke 12:11–12). With Paul, they should maintain their innocence (Acts 25:8) and with Peter and John they should 'obey God rather than human beings' (Acts 4:19; 5:29; my trans.).

Third, Luke underlines the supremacy of Jesus over Caesar. Luke's prominent use of 'lord', 'king' (esp. Acts 17:7) and 'saviour' of Jesus is highly suggestive in this regard, for it highlights that Jesus, not Caesar, truly reigns. Thus – and supremely – the unjust execution of Jesus, in which both Jewish and Roman authorities were complicit, was overcome and reversed by God in the resurrection.[108] Luke also draws attention to God's

---

[107] Cf. Bond, *Pontius Pilate*, 147.

[108] Note the use of passive voice forms of ἐγείρω with God as subject and Jesus as direct object in evangelistic speeches; e.g. Acts 3:15; 4:10; 5:30; 13:30.

reassurances to Paul that he will stand before the emperor (Acts 23:11; 27:23–4) – both occasions coming when Paul's circumstances would lead Luke's readers to think the opposite might be the case. The evident climax of the book at Paul's arrival in Rome underlines how God has kept his word. Throughout Luke-Acts God works his purposes out, whether or not he receives human co-operation, and those purposes are not ultimately frustrated; hence (for example) he rescues Paul and Silas from prison in Philippi (Acts 16:25ff.) and enables Stephen to be faithful to death (Acts 7). The greatness of God's power is an encouragement to Luke's readers to keep trusting God, for he is at work and his purposes will come to fruition in spite of human opposition.

In sum, Luke offers his readers a strategy of critical distance from the empire. He thus falls at *both* ends of the spectrum between Romans 13 and Revelation 13 that I sketched. Where co-operation and mutual respect are possible, Christians should do nothing to harm those; where the empire or its representatives turn against the church, the Christian stance is to be twofold: to call the state back to its former ways and to bear faithful witness to Jesus. The church is to live in the knowledge that, just as its Lord suffered injustice from the empire and was vindicated, so the church of the Lord will be able to withstand by the same 'good confession'.

Bibliography

Alexander, Loveday, *The Preface to Luke's Gospel: Literary Convention and Social Context in Luke 1.1–4 and Acts 1.1* (SNTSMS 78; Cambridge: Cambridge University Press, 1993)

Barclay, John M.G., 'Mirror-reading a Polemical Letter: Galatians as a Test Case', *JSNT* 31 (1987), 73–93

—, review of Richard J. Cassidy, *Society and Politics in the Acts of the Apostles* (Maryknoll, NY: Orbis Books, 1987), *SJT* 42 (1989), 577–9

Barrett, C.K., *A Critical and Exegetical Commentary on the Acts of the Apostles*, vol. II: *Introduction and Commentary on Acts XV–XXVIII* (ICC; Edinburgh: T. & T. Clark, 1998)

—, *Luke the Historian in Recent Study* (London: Epworth Press, 1961)

Bauckham, Richard (ed.), *The Gospels for All Christians* (Edinburgh: T. & T. Clark / Grand Rapids: Eerdmans, 1997)

—, 'Response to Philip Esler', *SJT* 51 (1998), 249–53

Beasley-Murray, George R., *John* (WBC 36; Dallas, TX: Word Books, 1987)

Bond, Helen K., *Pontius Pilate in History and Interpretation* (SNTSMS 100; Cambridge: Cambridge University Press, 1998)

Borg, Marcus J., *Conflict, Holiness and Politics in the Teachings of Jesus* (Lewiston, NY: Edwin Mellen Press, 1984)

Brown, Raymond E., *The Birth of the Messiah* (ABRL; London: Geoffrey Chapman, 1993)

Bruce, F.F., *The Book of Acts* (NICNT; Grand Rapids: Eerdmans, rev. edn, 1988)

—, *Paul: Apostle of the Free Spirit* (Exeter: Paternoster Press, 1977)

—, 'Render to Caesar', in Ernst Bammel and C.F.D. Moule (eds.), *Jesus and the Politics of His Day* (Cambridge: Cambridge University Press, 1984)

Burton, G.P., 'Proconsuls, Assizes and the Administration of Justice under the Empire', *JRS* 65 (1975), 92–106

Cadbury, Henry J., *The Making of Luke-Acts* (1927; London: SPCK, repr., 1958)

—, 'Some Foibles of New Testament Scholarship', *JBR* 26 (1958), 213–16

Carson, D.A., *The Gospel according to John* (Leicester: IVP / Grand Rapids: Eerdmans, 1991)

Cassidy, Richard J., *Jesus, Politics, and Society: A Study of Luke's Gospel* (Maryknoll, NY: Orbis Books, 1978)

—, *Society and Politics in the Acts of the Apostles* (Maryknoll, NY: Orbis Books, 1987)

Conzelmann, Hans, *Acts of the Apostles* (Hermeneia; Philadelphia: Fortress Press, 1987)

—, *The Theology of St Luke* (London: Faber & Faber, 1960)

Deissmann, Adolf, *Light from the Ancient East: The New Testament Illustrated by Recently Discovered Texts of the Graeco-Roman World* (London: Hodder & Stoughton, 1927[4])

Derrett, J. Duncan M., 'Luke's Perspective on Tribute to Caesar', in Richard J. Cassidy and Philip J. Scharper (eds.), *Political Issues in Luke-Acts* (Maryknoll, NY: Orbis Books, 1983)

Dunn, James D.G., *The Acts of the Apostles* (Epworth Commentaries; London: Epworth Press, 1996)

—, 'ΚΥΡΙΟΣ in Acts', in James D.G. Dunn (ed.), *The Christ and the Spirit: Collected Essays of James D.G. Dunn*, vol. 1: *Christology* (Edinburgh: T. & T. Clark / Grand Rapids: Eerdmans, 1998)

Easton, Burton Scott, *Early Christianity: The Purpose of Acts and Other Papers* (Greenwich, CT: Seabury Press, 1954)

Edwards, Douglas R., 'Surviving the Web of Roman Power: Religion and Politics in the Acts of the Apostles, Josephus, and Chariton's *Chaereas and Callirhoe*', in Loveday Alexander (ed.), *Images of Empire* (JSOTSup 122; Sheffield: JSOT Press, 1991)

Esler, Philip F., 'Community and Gospel in Early Christianity: A Response to Richard Bauckham's *Gospels for All Christians*', *SJT* 51 (1998), 235–48

—, *Community and Gospel in Luke-Acts: The Social and Political Motivations of Lucan Theology* (SNTSMS 57; Cambridge: Cambridge University Press, 1987)

Evans, Christopher F., *Saint Luke* (London: SCM Press, 1990)

Fitzmyer, Joseph A., *The Acts of the Apostles: A New Translation and Commentary* (AB 31; New York: Doubleday, 1998)

—, *Luke I–IX*, (AB 28; Garden City, NY: Doubleday, 1981)

—, *Luke X–XXIV* (AB 28A; Garden City, NY: Doubleday, 1985)

Franklin, Eric, *Christ the Lord* (London: SPCK, 1975)

French, David, 'Acts and the Roman Roads of Asia Minor', in David W.J. Gill and Conrad H. Gempf (eds.), *The Book of Acts in its Graeco-Roman Setting* (A1CS 2; Grand Rapids: Eerdmans / Carlisle: Paternoster Press, 1994)

Gasque, W.W., *A History of the Criticism of the Acts of the Apostles* (Grand Rapids: Eerdmans, 1975)

Gill, David W.J., 'Achaia', in David W.J. Gill and Conrad H. Gempf (eds.), *The Book of Acts in its Graeco-Roman Setting* (A1CS 2; Carlisle: Paternoster Press / Grand Rapids: Eerdmans, 1994)

—, 'Macedonia', in David W.J. Gill and Conrad H. Gempf (eds.), *The Book of Acts in its Graeco-Roman Setting* (A1CS 2; Carlisle: Paternoster Press / Grand Rapids: Eerdmans, 1994)

—, 'The Roman Empire as a Context for the New Testament', in Stanley E. Porter (ed.), *Handbook to Exegesis of the New Testament* (New Testament Tools and Studies 25; Leiden: E.J. Brill, 1997)

Gill, David W.J., and Conrad H. Gempf (eds.), *The Book of Acts in its Graeco-Roman Setting* (A1CS 2; Carlisle: Paternoster Press / Grand Rapids: Eerdmans, 1994)

Green, Joel B., *The Death of Jesus: Tradition and Interpretation in the Passion Narrative* (WUNT 2.33; Tübingen: J.C.B. Mohr [Paul Siebeck], 1988)

—, *The Gospel of Luke* (NICNT; Grand Rapids: Eerdmans, 1997)

Green, Michael, *Evangelism in the Early Church* (London: Hodder & Stoughton, 1970)

Haenchen, Ernst, *The Acts of the Apostles* (Oxford: Basil Blackwell, 1971)

Hanson, R.P.C., *The Acts* (New Clarendon Bible; Oxford: Clarendon Press, 1967)

Hart, H. StJ., 'The Coin of "Render unto Caesar ..."' (A Note on Some Aspects of Mark 12:13–17; Matt. 22:15–22; Luke 20:20–26)', in Ernst Bammel and C.F.D. Moule (eds.), *Jesus and the Politics of His Day* (Cambridge: Cambridge University Press, 1984)

Hemer, Colin J., and Conrad H. Gempf (ed.), *The Book of Acts in the Setting of Hellenistic History* (WUNT 49; Tübingen: J.C.B. Mohr [Paul Siebeck], 1989)

Heumann, C.A., 'Dissertatio de Theophilo, cui Lucas historiam sacram inscripsit', *Bibliotheca Historico-Philologico-Theologica, Class. IV* (Bremen, 1720), 483–505

Hoehner, Harold W., *Herod Antipas* (SNTSMS 17; Cambridge: Cambridge University Press, 1972)

Horsley, G. H. R., *New Documents Illustrating Early Christianity*, vol. 3 (North Ryde, NSW: Macquarie University, 1983)

Jeremias, Joachim, *The Eucharistic Words of Jesus* (London: SCM Press, 1966)

Jervell, Jacob, *The Theology of the Acts of the Apostles* (New Testament Theology; Cambridge: Cambridge University Press, 1996)

Johnson, Luke T., *The Acts of the Apostles* (Sacra Pagina 5; Collegeville: Liturgical Press, 1992)

Jones, A.H.M., *The Greek City from Alexander to Justinian* (Oxford: Clarendon Press, 1940)

Jones, D.L., 'The Title ΚΥΡΙΟΣ in Acts', *SBLSP* II (1974), 85–101

Kinman, Brent, *Jesus' Entry into Jerusalem in the Context of Lukan Theology and the Politics of His Day* (AGJU 28; Leiden: E.J. Brill, 1995)

Lacey, W.K., and B.W.J.G. Wilson, *Res Publica: Roman Politics and Society according to Cicero* (London: Oxford University Press, 1970)

Lewis, Naphtali, and Meyer Reinhold (eds.), *Roman Civilization: Selected Readings, vol. II: The Empire* (Records of Civilization: Sources and Studies 45; New York: Columbia University Press, 1955)

Lintott, Andrew, *Imperium Romanum: Politics and Administration* (London: Routledge, 1993)

Macro, Anthony D., 'The Cities of Asia Minor under the Roman Imperium', *ANRW* II.7.2 (1980), 658–97

Maddox, Robert, *The Purpose of Luke-Acts* (Edinburgh: T. & T. Clark, 1982)

Marshall, I. Howard, *The Gospel of Luke: A Commentary on the Greek Text* (NIGTC; Exeter: Paternoster Press, 1978)

—, *Luke: Historian and Theologian* (Exeter: Paternoster Press, 1970)

Millar, Fergus, *The Roman Empire and its Neighbours* (London: Duckworth, 1981²)

Murphy-O'Connor, Jerome, OP, *Paul: A Critical Life* (Oxford: Clarendon Press, 1996)

Nelson, Peter K., *Leadership and Discipleship: A Study of Luke 22:24–30* (SBLDS 138; Atlanta: Scholars Press, 1994)

Nolland, John, *Luke 1–9:20* (WBC 35A; Dallas, TX: Word Books, 1989)

—, *Luke 18:35–24:53* (WBC 35C; Dallas, TX: Word Books, 1993)

O'Toole, Robert F., SJ, 'Luke's Position on Politics and Society in Luke-Acts', in Richard J. Cassidy and Philip J. Scharper (eds.), *Political Issues in Luke-Acts* (Maryknoll, NY: Orbis Books, 1983)

—, review of Richard J. Cassidy, *Society and Politics in the Acts of the Apostles* (Maryknoll, NY: Orbis Books, 1987), *Bib* 70 (1989), 424–8

Oakes, Peter, *Philippians: From People to Letter* (SNTSMS 110; Cambridge: Cambridge University Press, 2001)

Page, Sydney H.T., 'The Authenticity of the Ransom Logion (Mark 10:45b)', in R.T. France and David Wenham (eds.), *Gospel Perspectives: Studies of History and Tradition in the Four Gospels*, vol. 1 (Sheffield: JSOT Press, 1980)

Peterson, David, 'The Motif of Fulfilment and the Purpose of Luke-Acts', in Bruce W. Winter and Andrew D. Clarke (eds.), *The Book of Acts in its Ancient Literary Setting* (A1CS 1; Carlisle: Paternoster Press / Grand Rapids: Eerdmans, 1993)

Rapske, Brian M., *The Book of Acts and Paul in Roman Custody* (A1CS 3; Carlisle: Paternoster Press / Grand Rapids: Eerdmans, 1994)

Reynolds, Joyce, 'Cities', in David C. Braund (ed.), *The Administration of the Roman Empire 241BC–AD193* (Exeter Studies in History 18; Exeter: University of Exeter Press, 1988)

Ringe, Sharon H., *Jesus, Liberation, and the Biblical Jubilee* (Overtures to Biblical Theology 19; Philadelphia: Fortress Press, 1985)

Robbins, Vernon K., 'Luke-Acts: A Mixed Population Seeks a Home in the Roman Empire', in Loveday Alexander (ed.), *Images of Empire* (JSOTSup 122; Sheffield: JSOT Press, 1991)

Sanders, E.P., *Paul* (Past Masters; Oxford: Oxford University Press, 1991)

Sanders, Jack T., *The Jews in Luke-Acts* (London: SCM Press, 1987)

Schürer, Emil, Geza Vermes and Fergus Millar, *The History of the Jewish People in the Age of Jesus Christ (175 BC–AD 135)*, vol. 1 (Edinburgh: T. & T. Clark, rev. edn, 1973)

Shelton, Jo-Ann, *As the Romans Did: A Sourcebook in Roman Social History* (Oxford: Oxford University Press, 1998²)

Soards, Marion L., *The Passion according to Luke: The Special Material of Luke 22* (JSNTSup 14; Sheffield: JSOT Press, 1987)

Squires, John T., *The Plan of God in Luke-Acts* (SNTSMS 76; Cambridge: Cambridge University Press, 1993)

—, 'The Plan of God in the Acts of the Apostles', in I. Howard Marshall and David Peterson (eds.), *Witness to the Gospel: The Theology of Acts* (Grand Rapids: Eerdmans, 1998)

Tajra, Harry W., *The Trial of St Paul: A Juridical Exegesis of the Second Half of the Acts of the Apostles* (WUNT 2.35; Tübingen: J.C.B. Mohr [Paul Siebeck], 1989)

Tannehill, Robert C., *The Narrative Unity of Luke-Acts: A Literary Interpretation*, vol. 1: *The Gospel according to Luke* (Philadelphia: Fortress Press, 1986)

Taylor, Vincent, *The Passion Narrative of St Luke* (SNTSMS 19; Cambridge: Cambridge University Press, 1972)

Thompson, Michael B., 'The Holy Internet: Communication between Churches in the First Christian Generation', in Richard Bauckham (ed.), *The Gospels for All Christians: Rethinking the Gospel Audiences* (Edinburgh: T. & T. Clark / Grand Rapids: Eerdmans, 1998)

Trebilco, Paul R., 'Asia', in David W.J. Gill and Conrad H. Gempf (eds.), *The Book of Acts in its Graeco-Roman Setting* (A1CS 2; Carlisle: Paternoster Press / Grand Rapids: Eerdmans, 1994)

Walaskay, Paul W., *And So We Came to Rome* (SNTSMS 49; Cambridge: Cambridge University Press, 1983)

Walton, Steve, *Leadership and Lifestyle: The Portrait of Paul in the Miletus Speech and 1 Thessalonians* (SNTSMS 108; Cambridge: Cambridge University Press, 2000)

—, 'Where Does the Beginning of Acts End?' in J. Verheyden (ed.), *The Unity of Luke-Acts* (BETL 142; Leuven: Peeters, 1999)

Weatherly, Jon A., *Jewish Responsibility for the Death of Jesus in Luke-Acts* (JSNTSup 106; Sheffield: Sheffield Academic Press, 1994)

—, 'The Jews in Luke-Acts', *TynBul* 40 (1989), 107–17

Wengst, Klaus, *Pax Romana and the Peace of Jesus Christ* (Philadelphia: Fortress Press, 1987)

Winter, Bruce W., *Seek the Welfare of the City: Christians as Benefactors and Citizens* (First-Century Christians in the Graeco-Roman World; Carlisle: Paternoster Press / Grand Rapids: Eerdmans, 1994)

Witherington, Ben, III, *The Acts of the Apostles: A Socio-Rhetorical Commentary* (Carlisle: Paternoster Press / Grand Rapids: Eerdmans, 1998)

Wright, N.T., *Jesus and the Victory of God* (Christian Origins and the Question of God, vol. 2; London: SPCK, 1996)

—, *The New Testament and the People of God*; (Christian Origins and the Question of God, vol. 1; London: SPCK, 1992)

2

Luke's Story of Paul's Reception in Rome

Conrad Gempf

The Questions

The discontinuity between our questions and those of the author of Luke-Acts is perhaps nowhere more apparent than at the end of the book. It is a commonplace now to say that authors, even would-be historians, are not closed-circuit TV cameras, objectively recording everything that happens within their field of vision. Authors make choices.

The ending of the book of Acts has long attracted attention because it leaves out the trial in Rome. If Luke *had* included the trial, every book on Acts would certainly talk about how the narrative, at least of the final third of the book, has been leading up to this climactic event.

There is now no shortage of explanations for the omission. But the scholarly world seems finally to have moved beyond mourning the missing trial and has begun to ask better questions about what *is* there. A historian might hope to retrieve some information about what the author thought the first-century Roman Christian and Jewish communities were like, but the better, if more fashionable, question is probably to ask what narratival purposes and concerns are being addressed and expressed in these stories of Paul's arrival and reception in Rome.

They are not stories that would strike one as atypical of Luke's double work: the themes are familiar and amply paralleled. And there are contemporary authors who have written about how what we have in Acts 28 together with Luke 1 or Acts 1 can be seen as framing the book as a whole.[1] But I do think it safe to say that if they had known only a copy of Acts that ended halfway through the final chapter, none of the scholars would have imagined it ending in precisely this way. Most of us might have guessed that on arriving in Rome, Paul would go to the synagogue first, but this tale is remarkable. Where are the Roman Christians? Why not show that Paul is not alone – that as he comes to the end of his tale there are those who will take over? Why not show the Gentiles being converted? At the beginning of Acts, in the Jewish capital, Peter makes thousands of Jewish converts with his speeches, why not end with Paul doing the same with Gentiles in their capital? Even apart from the missing trial, why squander one's precious papyrus on *this*?

In the past, many found the significance of this story in the condemnation of the Jews and the turning to the Gentiles without noticing how weak this condemnation and turning are. When we read some of the commentators, we can almost sense their disappointment: they must have fervently hoped for Luke to create (for it is all Lukan creation, is it not?) a rather more colourful gaggle of Jewish hoodlums, with gnashing teeth and pre-rent garments, skilled at one-handedly stopping both ears while throwing stones with the other hand. With a little luck, we might even have glimpsed a Clement holding coats in the wings. How tame and polite these Jews look when compared to others in Acts!

It must be admitted that one does not have to be a paid-up member of the Chelmsford Paul Seminar to sense that serious historical problems lurk here. Luke has told us in 18:2 that the Jews were at least temporarily expelled from Rome, and face-value readings of Suetonius and Orosius line up to suggest that the problem had something to do with disturbances caused by Christianity. How then is it possible for the Roman Jews to say that they do not know about Christianity?

Authors have choices and good authors make their decisions based on their goals and purposes. So what are Luke's purposes for the particular shape of this interview with the Jews? What is he trying to get across?

---

[1] See now esp. L. Alexander, 'Reading Luke-Acts from Back to Front', 419–46, citing 423–4, and the literature there cited.

The Narrative Features

The architecture of the story

In some respects our tale begins back in verse 14 with the arrival in Puteoli, the regular landing place for grain shipments bound for the capital. The first of two parties of Christian 'brothers' whom Paul meets are Puteoli dwellers, at whose house(s) Paul and his company stay for a week. He will later meet another party from Rome at the Forum of Appius and the Three Taverns. (And so Rome came to us!) Presumably during the week, word was sent by the Puteoli 'brothers' to those in Rome.

It is noteworthy that Luke's Paul accepts the hospitality of the Puteoli Christians without comment, yet is moved by the mere sight of the Roman Christians coming out to visit.[2] This may imply a degree of anxiety about the reception Luke's Paul would receive among Christians in the capital. Anxious as *we* are to hear more about the relationship between these two parties of Christians and the expectations on both sides, Luke tells us no more.

The narratological crafting of this last half chapter is little short of poetic. There is a stark contrast between the warmth of community and fellowship in verses 14 and 15 and the chained and guarded isolation of Paul in verse 16: after dwelling with the brothers there are the visitors on the road, and when *we* get to Rome, Paul is allowed to live by himself, with the soldier to guard him. Thus at the last even the travelling companions drop out of sight.

We should also note that although the narrator moves on to the story of Paul's interactions with the Roman Jews, verses 16 and 30 deliberately provide 'bookends' for that story, verse 30 reprising the 'allowed to live by himself' of verse 16. And it *is* a reprise rather than a mere resumption. Although more details are provided by the later verse, they are too repetitive to have been composed together with the Roman Jews story inserted later.[3]

---

[2] The decision of the Puteoli lot to billet at least the prisoner and perhaps the soldiers as well cannot really be judged an easier matter than travelling 30 or so miles to meet Paul. See Brian Rapske, *The Book of Acts and Paul in Roman Custody*, 205–6, 273–6.

[3] The 'he welcomed all who came' of v. 30 might be taken to betray ignorance of the story if Paul is interpreted as putting a final end to the

The story of Paul's interactions with the Jews inside the bookends[4] is normally seen as dividing conveniently into two subsections: the two days on which they meet.[5] The first occasion (vv. 17–22) is marked by a certain politeness and perhaps, as we shall see, even caution, whereas the second (vv. 23–8) is where the real business is usually thought by commentators to take place: the forceful preaching of the gospel and subsequent split between the Christians and the Jews. By contrast, however, to discuss the passage, one has in practice to split it into four subdivisions: (1) Paul's opening self-introduction, (2) the Jewish leaders' cautious invitation to Paul to speak further, (3) the episode of the uneven reaction to Paul's day of persuasion, and (4) Paul's citation of Isaiah 6 and application of it to the Roman Jews.

Once one goes to the trouble of dividing it so, one notices that, with the exception of the third of the four parts, the whole story is told not by the narrator but through exchanges of direct speech by the characters.[6] The effect of narrating something by indirect speech in a passage of otherwise direct speech is to de-emphasise that which is being summarised. We perhaps see this most clearly in the Council of Jerusalem of Acts 15. Luke wants to de-emphasise Paul's part in the church's decision not to require circumcision of the Gentiles; thus *Peter* is given a speaking part, *James* is given a speaking part, and Paul is merely said to *have spoken* about his ministry. In our passage, a significant missionary speech of Paul has been reduced to summary

---

[3] (*continued*) Jewish mission in v. 28, but ultimately this reconstruction cannot be maintained.

[4] Namely vv. 17–28; v. 29 is widely rejected as late. For another analysis of this structure see J. Dupont, 'La conclusion des Actes et son rapport à l'ensemble de l'ouvrage de Luc', 361–6, esp. 362–3.

[5] With the imprimatur of Hauser's magisterial study on the passage, virtually all the commentators since have so divided the section into these two parts, usually mentioning Hauser. Let me be no exception: H.J. Hauser, *Strukturen der Abschlusserzählung der Apostelgeschichte*, 18ff. In fact, however, commentators had been so dividing the passage long before, as, e.g., Bruce's 1954 commentary, 529, 531, shows.

[6] Interestingly, even Soards, in his monograph about direct speech in Acts, seems barely to notice this, referring instead to Hauser's subdivisions and dividing the speeches of Paul up even more finely (*The Speeches in Acts*, 130–3).

and indirect speech (as are, more understandably, the various objections and murmurs of the opponents). The reason for treating it so cannot be, of course, that Luke dislikes repetition. This is patently obvious not only from the rest of the book of Acts but also from the fact that the turn from the Jews to the Gentiles *is* judged suitable to relay in direct speech, despite several earlier remarks of Paul to this effect having featured much more recently in the book than any of the mission-preaching to Jews.

Resonance(s) with previous stories

This brings us naturally to a comparison with similar passages elsewhere in the book. In particular, we must look at the other 'from now on' passages in which Luke's Paul starts in his usual pattern of going directly to the synagogue first, and then in direct speech announces his intention to turn from the Jews to the Gentiles.

I have in mind Acts 18:6, but more especially the story about Pisidian Antioch in 13:46–8.[7] Both for the similarities and for the differences, this parallel to Acts 28 deserves a closer look than it normally receives. That the Acts 13 and 28 stories result in some Jews joining and some rejecting is *not* a significant parallel, since virtually every mission story has a similar result. More suspicious is the fact that they both take place on two separate days and both proceed by means of direct speech. Even though the Jews' 'lines' are extremely short, their speaking part in Acts 13 (as in ch. 28) indicates initial acceptance of Paul as a fellow Jew and constitutes an invitation to speak to them. As with our story, the third of the four subdivisions is narrative summary and indirect speech before the final 'from now on' routine in direct speech.

The pattern, it needs to be stressed, is neither an *exact* parallel nor as well marked as chapter 28, but it is suggestive. And perhaps the differences are even more significant than the similarities. In Pisidian Antioch, unlike Rome, the mission preaching of Paul is

---

[7] It probably does not need to be mentioned that despite words that sound descriptive of a permanent rift – 'since you repudiate [the message] … we are now turning to the Gentiles' (13:46) and 'From now on I will go to the Gentiles' (18:6) – in each case when Paul went to a new community he went straight to the synagogue (14:1; 18:19).

given in direct speech that appears to have been what Luke wants to emphasise: what Paul taught the Jews. The emphasis will later, however, lie elsewhere.

Although Hauser thinks it significant that in contrast to Acts 13 or 18 the Paul of Acts 28 does not go to the synagogue,[8] this is of course due to the length of the chain[9] rather than a deliberate and symbolic authorial choice. But is it as a result of not being on the Jews' 'home turf' that the reaction is not as violent as in Acts 13, where the Jews stirred up persecution and drove Paul and his companions out? They can throw him out of the synagogue, but they cannot throw him out of his own home – especially if he is chained to it. All they can do is leave!

There are interesting parallels in other stories as well. We have a similarly invisible community of Christians in the Lystra story, for instance. Thus in 14:8–18, a story that also revolves around acceptance and rejection, Luke does not make any mention at all of a Christian community being founded. Yet he knows of one and, although it does not come into his purposes during the story about Lystra, their presence becomes clear later when in Derbe Paul decides it will be a good idea to return to encourage the Christian communities and mentions Lystra along with Iconium (14:21–2; cf. 16:1–2).

Moving on from Lystra, Barrett makes reference to the other story in which Paul gives a mission speech to Gentiles: the Athens episode. Barrett notes the request to hear more (17:19–20) where the phrasing as well as the idea is like the Roman Jews' request in 28:22.[10] But there is another potentially significant parallel as well: the clear note of ambiguity in the request. As elsewhere, the result of the further conversation is going to be inconclusive and divisive. Sergius Paulus also famously requests more information, but his request is quite different and with a better outcome (13:7, 12).

Schneider notes that 'delivered … into the hands of the Romans' (28:17) finds a precedent in the prophecy of Agabus (21:11), who

[8] Hauser, *Strukturen*, 93–4.

[9] This holds, of course, even if one chooses to believe that the chain and wrist are the author's creation rather than related to a real-life referent.

[10] C.K. Barrett, *The Acts of the Apostles*, 2:1242.

predicted that the Jews would deliver Paul into the hands of the Gentiles.[11] Such a fate is, of course, reckoned to be a horrible one for any Jew to consider. The irony is that Paul *sought out* such deliverance!

Another resonance, which seems to have been missed by Hauser, is the way that Luke's Paul makes use of chains as a prop in his speech (28:20), something he also did when before King Agrippa (26:29). Being thus bound is normally a source of great shame,[12] and in first-century culture shame was a serious matter.[13] But willingness to suffer and to lose honour for the sake of a commitment was understood and respected by the Romans,[14] so that reference to his own chains was an ironic reference to a loss of status that he himself had chosen. In both passages a cosmopolitan reader in the first century would be amazed at how well respected even a *bound* Paul could be. With Agrippa, Paul has won this respect by his attitude and speech; with the Roman Jews, Luke allows his character to make the point forcefully that the positive regard despite the chains is due to a stronger common bond.[15]

Conclusions drawn from the narrative features

The once popular notion that Luke makes Paul the pioneer of Roman evangelism cannot be maintained.[16] In terms of the use of

---

[11] The phrase also brings to mind Luke 9:44 and 18:32 ('into the hands of the Gentiles') about Jesus' terrible fate. G. Schneider, *Die Apostelgeschichte*, 2:414, n. 29, also mentions Luke 24:7, 'into the hands of sinful men' (cf. Acts 2:23).

[12] As the author of 2 Tim. 2:9 feels: 'for which I suffer hardship, even to the point of being chained like a criminal'. See Rapske, *Custody*, esp. 283–98.

[13] Ibid. 285–7, and the literature there cited.

[14] See, e.g., the description of the gladiatorial *sacramentum* as a willing embrace of being bound and beaten, and losing status as a 'prerequisite for courage' in Carlin A. Barton, *The Sorrows of the Ancient Romans*, 46, 47.

[15] Rapske sees the situation in historical rather than narrative terms, but correctly reads the ambiguity and irony of the situation. The chains could be for the Christians on the way to Rome, and for the Jews in Rome, an offence. Instead they are challenged to see it as a symbol of Paul's struggle alongside them. 'It is because of the hope of Israel' (*Custody*, 310).

[16] See, typically, Ernst Haenchen, *The Acts of the Apostles*, 729–31: 'But

indirect speech for the third of four subsections and in the light of the parallels with the other 'from now on' passages, it is clear that our story is told in such a way as to de-emphasise precisely that section that deals with the evangelism. Instead, the story seems to be about the connection and subsequent disconnection of Paul with Judaism.

Narratival/Rhetorical Protestations of Innocence and Ignorance

Paul avows innocence (vv. 17b–20)

The first of the four subsections runs from verses 17 to 20. Although the speech contains the seemingly familiar salutation ἄνδρες ἀδελφοί,[17] Luke has Paul begin the speech ἐγώ ἄνδρες ἀδελφοί, which we have not seen before in Acts.[18] This is unlikely to be mere stylistic variation: in his more desparate defence before the Sanhedrin, Luke's Paul stays with the formula ἄνδρες ἀδελφοί, ἐγώ twice within the space of six verses (23:1, 6) where we should expect stylistic variation.[19]

Whether the form here is deliberate and significant or not, it does point to the unusual character of this mini-speech, which

---

[16] (*continued*) why … did Luke present Paul's activities in Rome in this unhistorical manner? … to make Paul appear in Rome also conducting a mission to the Jews.'

[17] Interestingly, the Jews are addressed as brothers several times by Luke's Paul (and the other Christians), whereas when Paul addressed the Gentiles aboard the ship in the previous chapter, he used merely ἄνδρες, (27:21). But even more interestingly, in the only direct speech directed at Christians, Paul begins the speech with the second-person plural pronoun rather than ἄνδρες ἀδελφοι, as we might have expected (and which Peter and James used in speeches at Jerusalem).

[18] The closest parallel may be 2:37, where the repentant Jews put the 'what should we do?' ahead of the salutation 'brothers'. Cf. also 6:3.

[19] Witherington cites Longenecker with approval for seeing the ἐγώ before the salutation as a feature of forensic rhetoric 'indicating a personal *apologia* was to follow', but does not comment here or when he discusses the speech in ch. 26, why Paul does not use this form elsewhere (Ben Witherington III, *The Acts of the Apostles*, 796; cf. 687–90).

functions as almost a cross between a forensic defence[20] and a farewell speech. It is true we have neither the attempt to show recognition of the qualities of the 'judges' or audience, nor any specific denial of being guilty of anyone's blood. Yet quickly, Paul makes it clear that he has not done anything against the Jewish people or customs. He stops short of making the same claim about the Romans and their customs, however, saying in verse 18 no more than that the Romans agreed with him that there seemed to be no charges worthy of death. This is as we would expect any Jew to argue, but it is extremely interesting that Luke misses a chance to have Paul say that he is guilty of no Roman crime. Even so, the focus on Jewish customs would form an effective if indirect defence to Roman ears, stressing again that this is an internal Jewish matter on which the Romans have had to make a ruling not because the accusations have anything to do with them, but rather to see to a fair trial. No Roman laws were under threat, but Roman order and justice had to be seen to be ensured.

The statement 'I was forced to appeal to Caesar' (v. 19) has been passed over far too lightly in the literature. In reference to other passages, Rapske has pointed out clearly that the ambiguous status resulting from Paul's 'dual citizenship' appears to have caused confusion in several situations. People started treating him one way and then, when he revealed his citizenship, found they had to be much more careful of him.[21] Curiously, Rapske does not seem to notice that Paul's statement here in chapter 28 would have caused a similar feeling of political vertigo.[22] The Jews might have

---

[20] See now the fascinating discussion in S.C. Winter, 'Παρρησια in Acts', 185–202, esp. 198, 200–201, on legal language and public and private domains.

[21] The clearest examples are the Philippian incident, when Paul could demand an apology of those who had dismissively had him stripped, beaten and thrown into the inner prison (16:22–4, 37–9) and the Jerusalem incident in 22:19–29, written up with such typical political spin by Claudius Lysias in 23:27 'I … rescued him, having learned that he was a Roman'. See Rapske, *Custody*, 129–34, 140–9, and his ch. 4 on Paul's citizenship.

[22] Nor, curiously, does this part of the verse feature in Lentz's book about Paul's high social status, despite the importance he places on the 'appeal' (John C. Lentz Jr, *Luke's Portrait of Paul*, esp. 166–70).

thought they were talking with merely another 'brother'. Suddenly he calmly relates that when in trouble, he himself is in a position to demand a decision from the very top, from the emperor himself! Their view of him must suddenly change. Who is this whom even the winds, waves and Romans obey? This is no poor fellow Jew somehow captured and to be tried by the Romans, but someone who is being tried *by his own choice*, and using the privileges of a Roman! Luke has not given the Jews any opportunity to express an opinion about Paul yet in this story, but has tipped his hand here so that they now know that Paul is not a tourist in the great city of Rome – he is a citizen, and is thereby likely to have connections as good as, or even better than, they themselves have.[23]

Even without this, Rapske *does* note the sense of menace behind Paul's pledge that he has not come to Rome with any charge to bring against his own people (v. 19). Thus Rapske writes, '[this] statement [was] surely calculated to allay Roman Jewish concerns [and] makes little or no sense unless it is assumed that behind it lies something more than mere bravado … [W]hat seems to be present is the real prospect of Paul's doing serious damage … Paul is implying that he could launch a successful countersuit'.[24]

In his recent commentary, Walaskay brings up another matter, the deputations that had arrived from time to time in Rome from

---

[23] The status of the Jewish population of Rome is still a source of controversy, and their fortunes seemed to rise and fall, suggesting at least insecurity. Clearly many Roman Jews had been brought in as slaves after the intervention of Pompey in 63 BC, but these were enemies only because of the Jewish faction they backed, rather than because they were Jews *per se*. Pompey intervened in favour of Hyrcanus II and Antipater and, under Antipater and Herod, the Jewish nation were regarded as 'friends and allies' of a rather bewildering succession of powerful factions in Rome. But even here, the adroit manoeuvrings of the Herods kept them sailing close to the wind, and to a large extent, the perception of Jews living in Rome must have been affected. See John M.G. Barclay, *Jews in the Mediterranean Diaspora*, 289ff. See also n. 27 below on the so-called *religio licita* status.

[24] Rapske, *Custody*, 188–9.

Palestine to complain about this ruler or that policy, and it may well be that Paul was disavowing such a mission.[25]

We have already had occasion to mention the chains to which Paul refers in the next verse. The status implication of these is to be contrasted with the status revelation of Paul's ability to appeal to Rome; but more directly in the verse, the chains of Rome are contrasted with the hope of Israel. As Marshall writes, 'It was for being a loyal Jew, as he saw it, that Paul was wearing a Roman fetter, and this was surely something that demanded the attention of the Jews.'[26] Again, I add, it is for being a loyal Jew, and despite being a Roman citizen, that Paul finds himself thus. And yet he makes no complaint about Roman justice, but implies only that he has no immediate legal intentions against the Jewish people. All in all, Luke's Paul presents the Roman Jews with a complex political situation.

The Jews avow ignorance of Paul (v. 21)

Now it is the Jews' turn to speak, but what can they say? Before hearing Paul they could have comforted him and commiserated about the poor treatment of Jews by the Romans,[27] although it

---

[25] Paul W. Walaskay, *Acts*, 243. Although Walaskay does not here give the references, he is no doubt thinking of Philo's *Embassy to Gaius*, written about such a delegation to Rome that took place in perhaps 39 or 40 and the famous popular petitions against Herod's sons; Josephus, *Antiquities* 17.299–320; and *War* 2.80–100 (and perhaps also Luke 19:12–14).

[26] I.H. Marshall, *Acts*, 423.

[27] Recent scholarship has rightly reasserted itself against a technical status for *religio licita*, a modern rather than ancient phrase used to describe the way that Jewish practices were tolerated even where they must have caused friction with the authorities. The example of this that probably sparked the phrase was the way that Jewish synagogues were an exception to the tightening of restrictions against public meetings under Julius Caesar. Jews were certainly not allowed to do whatever they liked. Roman emperors felt it necessary to take disciplinary steps against the Jewish population of Rome on several occasions. Claudius, who had died only about six years before Paul's arrival in Rome, seems to have taken severe action on two occasions: first in AD 41, when he did not exile the Jews, but banned their meetings (Dio Cassius 60.6.6), and then again in AD 49, at which point he

might not be wise to make such statements too vehemently in the hearing of the guard to whom Paul was chained. Now, however, it appears that they are supposed to be on the other side of this matter, yet they will not be too interested in making an enemy of this man.

When in doubt, avoid taking sides, especially if you can justify the avoidance. What Luke has them say first is that they have no orders or reports (or even rumours) specifically about Paul. It is not difficult to believe this. Paul has only just arrived in Rome and the circumstances of his trip make it unlikely that any other ship would have reached Rome before he got there. Haenchen admits this, but still thinks 'unbelievable' that the Jews have not heard *anything* about Paul. He cites Acts 21:21 about what he calls 'Jewish charges against Paul', which he believes *must* have found their way to Rome. But he does not mention here that these are charges made by Jewish Christians.[28]

---

[27] (*continued*) does appear to have resorted to banishment (Suetonius, *Claudius* 25.4). G. Lüdemann, *Paul, Apostle to the Gentiles*, 162–71, and L.H. Feldman, *Jew and Gentile in the Ancient World*, 303–4, believe that Dio and Suetonius are writing contradictory accounts of the same event in 41, and indeed the Dio passage does look like a vehement clarification against a dialogue partner. But this requires dismissing the interlocking evidence of three sources – Suetonius (who on the hypothesis would be in error), Orosius (*Historiarum adversus Paganos*, 7.6.15–16, from whom we date the Suetonius event) and the Acts chronology (the circumstances of 18:2 would work well with a date of 49) – in favour of Dio Cassius. One can find valid reasons for being sceptical about any of these sources, but a theory that requires three out of four sources to be wrong cannot be regarded as safe. See n. 32 below and the literature there cited.

[28] Haenchen, *Acts*, 727, although in discussing 21:20–1 on pp. 608–9 he seems very clear that these are Jewish Christians and that the number of them (and therefore, it must follow, the importance of the outcry) is typical ancient exaggeration. He would be on more secure ground if, instead of citing 21:21, he had cited 21:28, where the Jews of Asia decry Paul to the crowd saying, 'This is the man who preaches to all men everywhere against our people, and the Law and this place.'

But there is no indication that anyone but these accusers from Paul's mission field recognise such a person. Instead they are mostly concerned about the next charge, the misunderstanding about Trophimus the Ephesian in the temple, as is shown by 21:28–9 and verses 22:21–2. The emphasis Luke gives to Paul's use of the Hebrew language to address them is probably

It is unsurprising that the Roman Jews have not heard about Paul. But it would be surprising if they had not heard about Christianity. Before passing on to that, however, we must notice that the implications of this verse spread wider than merely 'information about the lack of information'. They seem to be matching Paul's statement: he has no intention to press charges against the Jewish people. Part of what the Roman Jews are communicating is likely to be that, at present, they similarly have no intentions of taking part in pressing charges against him.[29] This is important, as it may even be one of the reasons why Paul is so anxious to see the Roman Jews. For if it is true that Paul is not to be underestimated, neither are they. Both sides are showing that their hands are empty of weapons, except of course for these chains!

The Jews' ignorance of Christianity (v. 22)

That the Jews next request more information about Christianity in such a congenial way is somewhat surprising to readers, especially twentieth-century commentators, who think Luke is making this scene up. However, such a request is not out of line with previous occasions in the book, such as the Gentiles in Athens, the case of Sergius Paulus (13:7), and Jews in Pisidian Antioch, as discussed above. Winter finds this description rather flattering for the Roman Jews, whom Luke appears to be portraying less negatively than Jews elsewhere, almost 'as philosophers'.[30]

---

[28] (*continued*) another indicator that the people thought that the incident was about an Asian Jew who was discovered by Asian Jews to be bringing an Asian Gentile into the temple. Thus Paul's defence is most effective at the beginning where he makes it clear that he speaks Hebrew and is not from Ephesus, but Tarsus and Jerusalem (21:40 – 22:3), and least successful when he returns to the subject of the Gentiles (22:21–2).

[29] Barrett (*Acts*, 1241–2) seems to have overreacted against this in arguing against the Jerusalem Jews dropping the prosecution. He has in any case misunderstood the more nuanced argument of Hemer regarding legislation against the default of accusers made law while Paul was in Rome awaiting trial rather than in place at the time of the interview with the Jews. See Colin Hemer, *The Book of Acts in the Setting of Hellenistic History*, 390–1.

[30] Again, he has in mind the parallels with Athens. See Winter, 'Παρρησια', 198–9.

It is usually regarded that where verse 21 is an avowal of ignorance regarding Paul specifically, verse 22 is an avowal of ignorance of Christianity more generally, given its reference to 'this sect' (αἵρεσις).[31] But two things must be noted. First, even in this verse, the main subject of the sentence is *Paul* and his views; the clause about 'this sect' is an elaboration on their alleged desire to hear more from Paul. And second, the Jews do not, in fact, plead ignorance of Christianity – quite the opposite. They would like to hear what Paul says not because of what they do not know, but because of what they *know*: that people everywhere speak against this sect.[32]

The ostensible 'disappearance' of the Christian community needs to be disentangled from this discussion. As I have shown above, the Christians have disappeared from other passages, without Luke hiding anything. Here too it is clear – from the way that the Roman Christians are not just mentioned but made a focal point in 28:15, and from the way that even the travelling companions melt

---

[31] Luke's use of the word αἵρεσις does not necessarily correspond to the English 'heresy' – see Acts 5:17, 15:5 and 26:5, where it is used of the Sadducees or Pharisees.

[32] Even this degree of detachment would be difficult, though not impossible, to reconcile with the facts if one took the line that the AD 49 expulsion of the Jews under Claudius was due to fighting between Jews and Christians. But there is a growing dispute about the proper interpretation of Suetonius, *Claudius* 25.4, and the related texts, even on a dating of 49. For a fair and concise discussion of the evidence and positions see Barclay, *Diaspora*, 303–6, and the literature there cited. If Suetonius's 'Chrestus' is a reference to Jesus, it still need not mean that there was open conflict between Jews and Christians; it might have been proselytisation of Romans that prompted Claudius to act against not only the Christians but the religion to which they were still regarded as belonging. But it is unclear that 'Chrestus' need refer to Jesus. While it is true that non-Christian writers frequently misspell 'Christus' as 'Chrestus', this is precisely because the latter was a common slave name, and if an unrelated 'Chrestus' had been involved in a serious incident connected with religion in the capital, the later confusion is all the more likely. Suetonius may be judged unlikely to have made the mistake himself, as he knows of Christianity, as evidenced in *Nero* 16.2, which speaks of that emperor punishing the Christians ('Christiani'). At that point Suetonius speaks of Christianity as a new superstition.

away – that Luke is not hiding the fact that there were Christians, as much as shooting a close-up of Paul in Rome.

The Jews want to know more about Paul's ideas, *without saying* that they do not know what Christians believe. Instead, they say that they know that it is spoken against by people everywhere (in contrast to Paul, of whom they have heard nothing spoken). The knowledge implied by this remark is substantial in quantity if not in quality: they have not heard merely *one* nasty story. For them to say, in the context of such an otherwise polite speech, that they know what 'people everywhere' think of Christians, surely means that Christianity must have been the subject of a number of conversations. Fitzmyer injects a hint of this in translating the phrase as 'For our part, we are anxious to hear you present your views, for we know full well about that sect, that it is denounced everywhere.'[33]

But who are these '[people] everywhere': Jews or Gentiles? The lawyer Tertullus also uses the word to bear the same sense of 'reputation' in Acts 24:3, about Felix's good reputation. In 1 Corinthians 4:17 Paul uses it about what is common knowledge among his communities, what he teaches everywhere (cf. Acts 21:28 where he is accused of teaching against Judaism everywhere). In Luke 9:6 a similar construct is used to refer to Jews in particular (the disciples go from village to village preaching and healing people everywhere), but in the Athens story (17:30, God has commanded people everywhere to repent) it clearly includes Gentiles. The phrase appears, in other words, to bear the same vagueness as the English 'everybody says so'.

What most scholars react against, however, is not what verse 22 says, or even what it implies about everyone's knowledge, but what it implies about the nature of the Jews' knowing. It is thought that, since they mention knowing that Christianity is spoken against, it means that that is the only thing they know and the only way they know it. Thus, for Haenchen, Luke's Jews know of Christianity 'only by repute'.[34] But, of course, this does not necessarily follow, especially in the course of *this particular* conversation. They are not, at this stage, having a conversation *about* the doctrines of

---

[33] Joseph A. Fitzmyer, *The Acts of the Apostles*, 789.

[34] The words of Barrett, whose recent commentary takes just this line (*Acts*, 1242).

Christianity. Rather, the discussion is about Paul's chains and the accusations against him. In such a conversation, the Jews struggle to remain neutral. They have no specific instructions against Paul but know merely that people accuse Christians. They are not replying with everything they know about Christianity; they are replying with everything they know about *accusations against* Christianity.

According to Haenchen, Schneckenberger 'once asserted that in reality the Jews had very precise information concerning Christianity. But they concealed their knowledge ...'[35] Bruce takes a similar, if not so bald, line in his commentary: 'on this occasion the leaders of the community judged it politic not to commit themselves on the subject'.[36] Haenchen replies that the Jews had no reason for such behaviour and that not a single syllable suggests that Luke knows the Jews to be holding anything back,[37] and none of the many new 1990s commentaries mentions the possibility, save Polhill, who speaks of the Jews 'maintaining distance', and who obliquely refers to Bruce's use of the word 'diplomacy'.[38]

Commentators, whose job is to comment primarily on what is in the text, are understandably reluctant to take up this suggestion about what is not. But the idea that the reader should feel that the Jews know more than they are saying has considerable merit. First, I have demonstrated that the dynamics of the situation (and this applies whether it be a historical one or merely a good dramatic composition) make such a reply at least not inappropriate. The discussion on day one concerns only the opposition to and accusations against Paul. Second, not only the history of Roman Jewry but Luke's own tale (18:2) would seem to make ignorance unlikely. Third, the character of the utterance itself lacks declarative clarity: as we have seen the Jews merely *imply* ignorance while talking about what they do know, which is different from their clearer plea

---

[35] See Haenchen, *Acts*, 727–8. He seems to give a page reference (86), but has not given it a footnote and no source attributed to Schneckenberger appears in his bibliography for either this passage or the previous ones back to the start of the chapter, nor in his initial lists of bibliographic abbreviations. Nor is there an index of authors.

[36] F.F. Bruce, *The Book of the Acts*, 506.

[37] Haenchen, *Acts*, 728, as if such things could be detected in syllables!

[38] See John B. Polhill, *Acts*, 540.

of ignorance about Paul. Fourth, it is not unlike Luke to allow his characters to make contrary-to-fact statements and implications. Sometimes he will parenthetically elucidate these, as with the similar interview in which the Athenians implied they were investigating but were really seeking titillation (17:19–21). But at other times he will let the words stand by themselves, as when these same Athenians say, 'We want to hear you again on this subject' (17:32). Luke knows that the Athenians have no real intention to make this come about, and the readers are probably intended to pick this up from his earlier comments about the Athenians and from the juxtaposition of Paul's dramatic 'but now' (17:30) and the Athenian 'not now'. Our passage holds similar clues. The nature of the theory makes proof virtually impossible, but the possibility that Luke pictures the Jews as holding some cards close to their chests must be given serious consideration.

To carry Fitzmyer's translation a bit further, might the request of the Jews be a reaction to Paul's declaration that it is for the hope of Israel that he is in chains? Is this a very different description of Christianity than they are used to? Instead of 'we don't know about Christianity' they might thus be saying something more along the lines of 'in chains for hope of Israel? Let us hear more, because this is not how Christianity has been explained to us! Everyone has spoken *against* it before.'

Whatever one makes of this, it is clear that Luke's Roman Jews are being extraordinarily accommodating. The use of the phrase 'this sect' for Christianity appears to show that the Roman Jews, at least at this stage, accept that Christianity is a sect within Judaism, even if it is not held in high esteem. One has only to think of the kinds of people who are accepted as Jews within Luke-Acts to realise how 'ordinary' even the Christians seem. Not only do the two main sects dealt with in the book differ more radically in terms of Scripture and practice than any two denominations within Christianity in what we regard as the modern era of plurality, but sorcerers like Elymas and the Keystone Cops-like act of the sons of Sceva seem to rate the adjective Jewish in first-century eyes. This use of αἵρεσις is one of the most commented-upon features of our passage, although few see the theme of acceptance as central or notice how this theme is graphically displayed in the Jews' willingness to return to speak further to Paul despite his chains.

Interestingly, the idea that these Roman Jews have information mainly in the form of rumours and reputation may qualify them as the kind of readers whom Luke claims to be addressing in the preface to his Gospel, so that this last story of the book reflects the purpose of the book as stated at the very beginning. The word κατηχέω in the preface is usually translated 'instructed' or 'taught', but it need not be. This translation reflects the usual view of Luke's audience as being primarily those who are Christians. If we translate it more along the lines of 'informed', we see a contrast: 'I have carefully examined everything from the beginning in order to write for you, excellent Theophilus, an ordered account so that you may know the truth regarding reports you have heard.' Luke is saying, 'You have heard scattered reports, Theophilus, but here is an ordered account of the whole thing.' Κατηχέω *is* used for instruction in Acts 18:25, but is also used unambiguously in the sense of being only partially 'informed' in Acts 21:21, 24.

Conclusion: Luke's Purpose and View

The purpose of the story of Jewish rejection

I have argued that this passage is to be seen primarily as a story about Christianity's status *vis-à-vis* Judaism, but what is Luke's point? What is he trying to say with the story? We must remember just how odd a choice this story is. So much must have happened to Paul in Rome; to select just this story and ignore the Christian communities in Rome, or Paul's trial, is remarkable.

Some have seen in this story an attempt by Luke to disown any continuing attempts to evangelise the Jews.[39] This too is completely unlikely. It makes light of the fact that this 'from now on' pattern

---

[39] See, e.g., Hans Conzelmann, *Acts of the Apostles*, 227; Roloff, *Apostelgeschichte*, 375; J.T. Sanders, *The Jews in Luke-Acts*, 298–9; and so too Hauser, *Strukturen*, 239–40. Jacob Jervell has a more nuanced view: J. Jervell, *The Unknown Paul*, 13–51. But see now Robert Tannehill, 'Rejection by the Jews and Turning to Gentiles', 83–101; Moessner, 'Paul in Acts', 96–104. Both of these argue persuasively against 20:28 as being 'paradigmatic and final', as Hauser has it.

occurs throughout the book, as, in the stories that follow, Paul always goes directly to the synagogue. As many have pointed out, there is no reason to believe that only Gentiles are meant by the word 'all' in Luke's closing statement that Paul welcomed and preached to 'all who came to see him'.

Others have tried to argue that this story is Luke's attempt to bamboozle the readers into believing that Paul was the founder of the church in Rome.[40] This can hardly be the case. Apart from what I have argued about the de-emphasis, and apart from the clear inclusion of Roman Christians earlier in the story, Paul is just not presented as successful enough. There are no Gentile converts portrayed and only a mixed Jewish response. The spotlight in the last verses is not on his converts but on his ability to preach relatively unhindered.

The story of the interaction between Paul and the Jewish leaders is not truly *about* evangelism at all.[41] That is why Luke has no trouble summarising that quarter of it. A more careful reading of the story, and one that attempts to read it in the context of the rest of the book, reveals that the message is that Christianity has not rejected the Jews, although the Jews have rejected Christianity, but they have done so only after initially conceding that Christianity is a sect of Judaism and that, despite the shame of his being in chains, the Jews regard Paul as 'one of them'.

We can agree, therefore, with Hauser that Paul and the Jewish leaders are representative, in Luke's mind, of Christianity and non-Christian Judaism respectively, and that the passage is a reply to the question 'Why has Israel rejected her hope?' The major differences between his view and mine are caused by (1) Hauser's decision that Luke's Paul is rejecting Jews as much, or more than, they are rejecting him, and (2) his assumption that a late-writing Luke would have seen Christianity as totally distinct from Judaism and thus have seen Paul the Christian, rather than Paul among his own people,

---

[40] We have seen that Haenchen, for instance, is of this persuasion. See n. 16 above.

[41] So also, with somewhat different conclusions, Loveday Alexander: 'The stress in ch. 28 is not so much on preaching the Gospel to the Romans (contrast the Athens scene of Acts 17) as an ongoing debate within the divided Jewish community' ('Reading Luke-Acts from Back to Front', 428).

the Jews.[42] On the first of these it is clear throughout the book that Luke is trying to convince the reader that Paul's turning to the Gentiles was *not* his own idea – that it was not something about which he had much choice. Paul did not summon the Gentiles in Rome, but was 'forced' to turn to them when the Jewish community rejected him.

But, having once said that, the emphasis in this story is much more finely nuanced, and Luke seems especially careful to point out to us that it is not that the Jews rejected Paul outright. They accept that Christianity is a sect of Judaism, albeit one spoken against; and they initially accept Paul as one of their own community, responding to his summons and returning to see him, although they clearly have been made aware of his chains and all that these imply. The rejection of the Jews, Luke wishes to stress, is a rejection from within. His point is that although Christians work among Gentiles, this is not a sign that they are deliberately outside Judaism.

Now what does all this imply about Roman Christianity in the first century? The answer, I am afraid, depends upon your view of when and for whom Acts was written. If, as I do, you believe that Acts was written early to a Roman audience of god-fearers and other interested, even curious, non-Christians, then this Lukan apology is most likely implying a Christian community that defies expectations (and sensibilities) by being largely Gentile at the time of writing. Further implied is that before Paul's arrival the Christian congregation was either too small to draw much attention, or else was primarily Jewish.

There are, I recognise, good reasons for thinking that Acts was written later and to a Christian audience. In such a situation, however, it is unlikely that Luke has to defend the move to a Gentile mission, which is no longer contrary to expectation. Rather, it must be that he is defending the mixed nature of the congregation, saying that, although the Jews as a congregation wound up rejecting us, it was not always the case, and significant numbers expressed their Judaism in Christianity even before the turn to the Gentiles.

A Luke writing early is passionately maintaining that the dispute between Judaism and Christianity is a dispute not between two separate institutions but is an internally Jewish dispute, despite

---

[42] Hauser, *Strukturen*, 235–40.

the appearance of the church as being Gentile in focus and/or composition. The phrase 'Paul and the Jews' for Luke means not 'our hero, Paul, and those other people', but 'Paul and his own people'. This misreading in Hauser and others is partly responsible for the common notion that Luke is anti-Semitic. Thus Luke is not saying, 'Here is why we hate those people'; instead, he is saying, 'Here is why our own people no longer embrace us.'

The purpose of the story of Jewish ignorance

Or perhaps instead of 'the story of Jewish ignorance' we should say 'the story of the *implication* of Jewish ignorance', for as we have seen, Luke's Jews stop short of actually claiming ignorance of Christianity the way that they claim ignorance about the details of Paul's case.

The motif works in Luke's favour in that it allows him to emphasise the Jews' initial acceptance of Paul and of Christianity. Their willingness to come back to hear him, despite his Christianity and despite his chains, allows Luke to show clearly that they have rejected Paul not because he is not Jewish but because they come to feel that his Judaism is not congenial to the Judaism of some of them.

Despite the historical difficulties, it is not necessary to believe that this is an entirely Lukan creation. Whatever decision one comes to about Suetonius's Chrestus, it is clear that the Jews are on rather insecure footing in Rome and simply cannot afford another riot.[43] There is some 'posturing' going on in the exchange between them, in which Paul promises that he has not come to press a complaint against other Jews, and they seem to indicate that they have no intention of taking up the charges against him. They *do* know Christianity, and their line of 'we have heard it spoken against' is a safely impersonal line to take in criticising someone.[44]

---

[43] Episodes such as the accusation in Philippi 'these men ... being Jews ...' (Acts 16:20–1), the riot in Ephesus (20:33–4) and the whipping of the Corinthian synagogue leader before Gallio (19:17) foreshadow for the reader concerns of which the Jewish leaders will not have needed to be reminded and which may have influenced their attitude towards Paul.

[44] K. Lake hints similarly when, in commenting on v. 19, he writes, 'hence, perhaps, the anxiety of the Roman Jews to dissociate themselves from the case' (*The Beginnings of Christianity*, 4:346).

Luke's view of the state of the communities in Rome

When we turn back to the questions most directly relevant to the matter of Roman Christianity, namely the state of the Christian and Jewish communities prior to Paul's arrival, we find that the major thing we learn about them is that both communities seemed to keep their heads down.

Despite the fact that the Christians, and even Paul's companions, disappear into the woodwork once Paul reaches Rome proper, there are tantalising clues about the believing community from the earlier appearance in the Forum of Appius and Three Taverns. To the extent one is willing to trust Luke, one can say that the pre-Pauline Christians appear to have formed a well-organised network, since they were able to get news from Puteoli to Rome in time for Christians to come out to meet Paul. Further, the fact that there were Christians whose situations were sufficiently flexible to allow them to make the journey at such short notice would suggest a community with at least some wealthy members.

Also, whether or not one agrees with my argument that what is classified as the ignorance of the Jews might be better classified as the restraint of the Jews, these Jews are sufficiently well behaved (even *after* a parting of ways) to make it unlikely that the Roman Christians have had a very serious or at least very seriously unpleasant impact on the Jewish community. These Jews are not rabidly anti-Christian. Yet we are left in no doubt that Rome is not neutral about Christians and Christianity. All the people speak ill of the new movement, even if no one knows quite what it really is.

Although the author grants them more time on stage, we learn less about the Jews with any certainty. Luke does not leave us with the impression of a disorganised Jewish community. That Paul can 'summon' the leaders of the Jews and have them arrive is impressive. As just mentioned, we also learn that Luke's view is that the Roman Jews did not start out as anti-Christian as we might have expected. Instead, to our surprise, they seem quite open and even interested, either genuinely or in terms of this posturing.

Authors have choices, and good authors make decisions based on a purpose for writing. Luke's main purpose in presenting and emphasising this episode must have to do with explaining both the real connection, but also the apparent disconnection, between Christianity and Judaism.

Bibliography

Alexander, Loveday, 'Reading Luke-Acts from Back to Front', in J. Verheyden (ed.), *The Unity of Luke-Acts* (Leuven: Leuven University Press, 1999)

Barclay, John M.G., *Jews in the Mediterranean Diaspora: From Alexander to Trajan (323 BCE – 117 CE)* (Edinburgh: T. & T. Clark, 1996)

Barrett, C.K., *The Acts of the Apostles*, vol. 2 (ICC; Edinburgh: T. & T. Clark, 1998)

Barton, Carlin A., *The Sorrows of the Ancient Romans: The Gladiator and the Monster* (Princeton: Princeton University Press, 1993)

Brawley, Robert L., *Luke-Acts and the Jews: Conflict, Apology and Conciliation* (SBLMS 33; Atlanta: Scholars Press, 1987)

Bruce, F.F., *The Book of the Acts* (NICNT; Grand Rapids: Eerdmans, 1988²)

Clarke, Andrew D., 'Rome and Italy', in C. Gempf and D. Gill (eds.), *The Book of Acts in its Graeco-Roman Setting* (A1CS 2; Grand Rapids: Eerdmans, 1994)

Conzelmann, Hans, *Acts of the Apostles*, trans. J. Limburg, A.T. Kraabel and D.H. Juel (Hermeneia; Philadelphia: Fortress Press, 1987 [Ger. 1972])

Dupont, Jacques, 'La conclusion des Actes et son rapport à l'ensemble de l'ouvrage de Luc', in J. Kremer (ed.), *Les Actes des Apôtres: Traditions, rédaction, théologie* (Leuven: Leuven University Press, 1978)

Feldman, Louis H., *Jew and Gentile in the Ancient World: Attitudes and Interactions from Alexander to Justinian* (Princeton: Princeton University Press, 1993)

Fitzmyer, Joseph A., *The Acts of the Apostles* (AB; London: Doubleday, 1998)

Haenchen, Ernst, *The Acts of the Apostles*, trans. B. Noble and G. Shinn (Oxford: Blackwell, 1971 [Ger. 1965])

Hauser, Hermann J., *Strukturen der Abschlusserzählung der Apostelgeschichte (Apg 28,16–31)* (AnBib 86; Rome: Biblical Institute Press, 1979)

Hemer, Colin, *The Book of Acts in the Setting of Hellenistic History* (WUNT 49; Tübingen: J.C.B. Mohr, 1989)

Jervell, J., *The Unknown Paul: Essays on Luke-Acts and Early Christian History* (Minneapolis: Augsburg, 1984)

Johnson, Luke Timothy, *The Acts of the Apostles* (Sacra Pagina; Collegeville: Michael Glazier, 1992)

Lake, K., *The Beginnings of Christianity*, vol. 4 (London: Macmillan, 1920–33)

Lentz, John C., Jr, *Luke's Portrait of Paul* (SNTSMS 77; Cambridge: Cambridge University Press, 1993)

Levinskaya, Irina, *The Book of Acts in its Diaspora Setting* (A1CS 5; Carlisle: Paternoster, 1996)

Lüdemann, Gerd, *Paul, Apostle to the Gentiles: Studies in Chronology*, trans. F. Stanley Jones (London: SCM, 1984)

Marshall, I.H., *Acts* (TNTC; Downers Grove: IVP, 1980)

Moessner, David P., 'Paul in Acts: Preacher of Eschatological Repentance to Israel', *NTS* 34 (1988), 96–104

Polhill, John B., *Acts* (New American Commentary; Nashville: Broadman, 1992)

Rapske, Brian, *The Book of Acts and Paul in Roman Custody* (A1CS 3; Carlisle: Paternoster / Grand Rapids: Eerdmans, 1994)

Roloff, J., *Die Apostelgeschichte* (NTD 5; Göttingen: Vandenhoeck & Ruprecht, 1981[17])

Sanders, Jack T., *The Jews in Luke-Acts* (London: SCM, 1987)

Schneider, G., *Die Apostelgeschichte*, vol. 2 (Freiburg: Herder, 1982)

Soards, M.L., *The Speeches in Acts: Their Content, Context and Concerns* (Louisville: Westminster / John Knox Press, 1994)

Tajra, Harry W., *The Martyrdom of St Paul* (WUNT 2.67; Tübingen: J.C.B. Mohr, 1994)

—, *The Trial of St Paul* (WUNT 2.35; Tübingen: J.C.B. Mohr, 1989)

Tannehill, Robert C., 'Rejection by the Jews and Turning to Gentiles: The Pattern of Paul's Mission in Acts', in Joseph B. Tyson (ed.), *Luke-Acts and the Jewish People: Eight Critical Perspectives* (Minneapolis: Fortress Press, 1988)

Tyson, Joseph B., *Images of Judaism in Luke-Acts* (Columbia: University of South Carolina Press, 1999²)

Walaskay, Paul W., *Acts* (Westminster Bible Companion; Louisville: Westminster / John Knox Press, 1998)

—, *And So We Came to Rome: The Political Perspective of St Luke* (SNTSMS 49; Cambridge University Press, 1983)

Wansink, Craig S., *Chained in Christ: The Experience and Rhetoric of Paul's Imprisonments* (JSNTSup 130; Sheffield Academic Press, 1996)

Winter, S.C., 'Παρρησια in Acts', in J.T. Fitzgerald (ed.), *Friendship, Flattery and Frankness of Speech: Studies on Friendship in the New Testament World* (Leiden: E.J. Brill, 1996)

Witherington, Ben, III, *The Acts of the Apostles: A Socio-Rhetorical Commentary* (Cambridge: Eerdmans, 1998)

3

Roman Law and Society in Romans 12–15

Bruce Winter

Roman law was constructed with a bias towards social privilege. Both in its criminal and civil spheres it unashamedly favoured those of superior social status, providing them with legal privileges and protection.[1] For example, because it operated on the basis of private and not public prosecutions, it was not possible to mount a case against certain categories of people. Proceedings could not be brought against a parent, a patron, a person of higher rank or either a magistrate or governor while in office, by children, clients who included freedmen, private citizens, those of inferior rank or officials of cities or leagues respectively.[2] The former groups operated with the full knowledge of their social privileges supported by legal immunity.[3]

How wide was their immunity? J. Crook's central thesis in *Roman Life and Law, 90 BC–AD 212* was that it is impossible to deal with Roman society and Roman law as if they were basically autonomous spheres in Rome or, we might add, in Roman colonies of the empire. Essential aspects of Roman society were consciously built on Roman law and operated on that basis. Unlike cultures before or after, citizens of Rome and Roman colonies scattered throughout the empire were aware of this important nexus and therefore were well informed on how their

---

[1] P. Garnsey, *Social Status and Legal Privilege in the Roman Empire*.

[2] Ibid. 182.

[3] For examples of this in relation to criminal and civil litigation in the Corinthian church see my *After Paul Left Corinth*, 50–1, 59–60.

rights and privileges were grounded in Roman law and how much of life was determined by it.[4]

The title of this chapter was framed recognising that reality. It deliberately reverses the order of A.N. Sherwin-White's excellent *Roman Society and Roman Law in the New Testament* in examining this portion of Romans.[5] He did not draw the attention of New Testament scholars to the wide parameters of life encompassed by Roman law: hence he re-enforced the general perception in New Testament studies that this much admired system of jurisprudence covered essentially criminal matters. While it was true that the Roman governor's *imperium* was concerned primarily with criminal law, it has meant that New Testament studies have not taken cognisance of the wider nexus between Roman law and Roman society.

Most importantly, Paul saw the Christians' response was to surrender to the will of God in the matters discussed in Romans 12–15, which were the antithesis to culturally determined conduct in Rome. The Christian community 'must not be fashioned by the present age' in which it lived (12:2). Given the widely held view of the superiority of *Romanitas* – even by some foreigners resident in the imperial capital[6] – Paul demanded the abandoning of certain cherished cultural norms that operated both inside and outside their community. His apostolic experience in the East of the empire, especially while residing in the Roman colony of Corinth, meant he was no stranger to the impact of *Romanitas* on Christian communities.[7]

It would be expected, therefore, that in chapters 12–15 Paul was assessing Roman cultural mores based on privileges and power

---

[4] J.A. Crook, *Roman Life and Law, 90 BC–AD 212*, 7–8, for a discussion of the penchant of Roman citizens for a knowledge of legal matters for this very reason.

[5] A.N. Sherwin-White, *Roman Society and Roman Law in the New Testament*. The title was to some extent misleading. He dealt with criminal jurisdiction and primarily the criminal cases of the Jews versus Jesus and Paul, as well as his critical observations concerning gospel studies from the perspective of a Roman historian, 186–93.

[6] D. Noy, *Foreigners at Rome*, 287, on integration on the part of some.

[7] He was well aware of the inroads of *Romanitas* in the Corinthian church. See my *After Paul Left Corinth*, 7–22.

enshrined in Roman law. It is being suggested that insufficient attention has been paid to the way Paul interacts with Roman society/law in the major section of ethical instruction in this letter. Here the will of God is spelt out in important areas of life, over against those based on Roman law, which enshrined established conventions for the privileged and regulated relationships between social inferiors and superiors.

He appeals for conduct, not based on privilege or lack of it, but on 'the mercies of God' discussed in chapters 9–11. Romans 12:1 clearly marks this connection with the use of 'therefore' (οὖν). They, and not Roman law, must form the motivation for conduct in the various spheres of life including a new approach to Jewish and Gentile Christian relationships in Rome, especially in the extremely complex situation that had arisen in chapters 14 – 15.

The purpose of this chapter then is to explore the impact of the rights and privileges on those aspects of life reflected in Romans 12–15. It will examine (1) Roman perceptions and Christian self-definition; (2) the privileged and one's *persona*, 12:3–21; (3) the privileged and *politeia*, 13:1-7; (4) the privileged and promiscuity, 13:8-14; and (5) the privileged and the powerless, 14–15. Whether Paul is to be seen as a social realist, a social conservative or a social critic of Roman law and society as he interacts with cultural issues affecting the Christian community in Rome, will be briefly canvassed in the conclusion on the basis of the preceding analysis.[8]

Roman Perceptions and Christian Self-definition

In view of the connection between Roman law and society, the first issue to explore is how others in Rome would have perceived the Christian community and how the Christians would have seen themselves. Such an exploration is important, given the fact that the latter were culturally programmed to be citizens of 'this age' before they became citizens of the kingdom of God. How did the former

[8] 'St. Paul as a Critic of Roman Slavery in 1 Corinthians 7:21–23', 339–54, especially 353–4 for my succinct observations of his critique of wider Roman cultural issues.

see themselves? They resided in a dynamic city where relationships with others were grounded in the privileges of Roman law. In subsequent sections the norms of 'this age' in Rome will be evaluated against 'the will of God'.

It is known how the Roman officials in Antioch, the capital of Syria and the seat of the imperial legate, defined the early followers of Christ – they were described as *Christianoi*. Acts 11:26 makes it clear that this was not a self-definition, but that the disciples were publicly known by this term.[9] E.A. Judge has drawn attention to the fact that 'The Greek-speaking synagogues in Rome used the Greek suffix -εσιοι in their names. The suffix *–ianus* [the Latin rendering of Χριστιανός] constitutes a political comment. It was not used for the followers of a god. It classifies people as partisans of a political or military leader, and is mildly contemptuous.' Judge believes that the term *Christianus* could have arisen 'from the question posed for Romans over the political loyalty of the followers of Christ'. He argues convincingly that the term was not a self-definition nor was it a Jewish designation, but a Roman one. He also believes that it helps explain the sharp retort of Agrippa to Paul in his attempt to persuade him to become a *Christianus*, given that the speech was made before the new Roman governor. It was in his Roman court in Caesarea Maritima, the capital of the Province of Judaea, that the resumed hearing against Paul took place in the presence of the dignitaries (Acts 26:28). Tacitus records the incident concerning the fire in Rome in Nero's Principate and refers to them as a class of men 'whom the crowd styled Christians' (*vulgus Christianos appellabat*).[10]

The only other piece of evidence of disciples of Christ being called Χριστιανοί in New Testament times is in 1 Peter written to Christians in Asia Minor. Again the term is used possibly as a charge made by outsiders. The recipients of the letter are assured that this was not shameful as, in first-century society, public

---

[9] F.F. Bruce, *The Acts of the Apostles*, 274.

[10] E.A. Judge, 'Judaism and the Rise of Christianity', 82–98, republished *TynBul* 45.2 (1994), 363, cites as an example 'The young knights whom Nero engaged to applaud his performances [were] dubbed "*Augustiani*",' Suetonius, *Nero* 25.1, Tacitus, *Annals* 15.14. J.W. Hargis, *Against the Christians*, 11, on the pejorative use of the term.

accusations were a means of humiliation[11] – 'if any one suffer as a Christian (ὡς Χριστιανός) let him not be ashamed' (4:16). Judge cites Trajan who, in the early second century, wrote of 'those who were brought before you as Christians', a name by which, at this time, they were also known.[12] That does not eliminate the political and derisory connotations attached to it in the early decades of the Christian church.

We also have evidence from the famous Pliny/Trajan official correspondence alluding to associations. It reveals an atmosphere where associations in his province had become the source of political agitation. As a result, during his governorship of Bithynia, Pliny had recourse to the emperor for advice on their activities on a number of occasions.[13] Trajan's response to the possibility of forming an association of fire-fighters in Nicomedia records the imperial view: 'When people gather together for a common purpose – whatever name we may give them and whatever function we may assign them – they soon become political groups.'[14] His second exchange of correspondence reveals Trajan's attitude: 'In other cities, however, which are subject to our laws, I would have all such societies of this nature [associations devoted to charity] prohibited.'[15] He had forbidden secret societies and made their formation a treasonable offence punishable by death.[16]

It is in this context that the correspondence about Bithynian Christians should be read. '[T]hey were accustomed to meet on a fixed day before dawn … and to bind themselves by an oath – not to commit some crime, but an oath not to commit theft, robbery, or adultery, not to break their word, and not to refuse to return a deposit when called upon.'[17] There were three types of associations

---

[11] R.A. Kaster, 'The Shame of the Romans', 1–19.

[12] Pliny the Younger, *Letters*, 10.97.

[13] Ibid. 10.96, 97.

[14] Ibid. 10.33, 34.

[15] Ibid. 10.92, 93, on clubs formed for charity purposes, citation from 10.93.

[16] Cf. ibid. 10.82, where Trajan was concerned that he would not want 'every slight offence' construed as 'an act of treason'.

[17] Ibid. 10.96. 93.

(*collegia*): funerary, religious and professional.[18] It is clear into which category outsiders would readily place the Christian community after observing their activities or hearing about them, however garbled the account.

How then would the Christian community have been perceived in Rome? The question needs to be posed in more general terms: How were any gatherings, and hence members of a defined group, including Jews, classified by the Romans, given their legal/cultural mindset? Evidence suggests that they would have been seen as an association, and the question would then have arisen whether it was an authorised or illegal one. In the Julian legislation Augustus moved to curb the political power of the associations that had formed in Rome. He perceived that they had become hotbeds of political activity and dissension. He stipulated that they had to secure, via him, the approval of the Roman Senate for their existence, and to do so they had to provide some public service.[19] As Cotter notes, this move 'ensured that the voluntary/private societies were conservative in character and *publicly* loyal to Augustus'.[20]

Augustus also prohibited associations meeting more than once a month, but in that move specifically exempted the Jewish 'association' so they could gather to observe their weekly sabbath. The fact that, for legal purposes, the latter group was perceived to

---

[18] For a discussion of these and the fact that the threefold classification was not that clear because of the place of cultic activities in them, see J.S. Kloppenborg, '*Collegia* and *Thiasoi*', ch. 2. The volume is a model of scholarship on the subject. On professional associations in the East see the important monograph by O.M. Van Nijf, *The Civic World of Professional Associations in the Roman East*.

[19] For an example of this see *CIL* VI no. 2193. 'For the association of bandsmen, who perform at public rites, whom the Senate permitted to meet, to be convened, to be assembled under the Julian law by the authority of Augustus for the sake of the games' (*Collegio symphoniacorum qui sacris publicis praestu sunt, quibus senatus c(oire) c(ogi) c(onvocari) permisit e lege Iulia ex auctoriatate Aug(usti) ludorum causa*). Cf. Suetonius, *Augustus* 32.

[20] W. Cotter, 'The Collegia and the Roman Law', 78. The method of securing approval was codified in the second century, Gaius, 'On the Provincial Edict', *Institutes* 3.

be an association, albeit a legal one, provides a clue as to how any group seen to be derived from it would be classed in Rome.[21]

The policy of Tiberius towards associations was reflected in the actions of his close friend Flaccus, Prefect of Egypt, who, according to Philo, banned all associations and clubs in Alexandria. All foreign cults, especially Egyptian and Jewish ones, were banned from Rome in AD 19.[22]

When Claudius 'disbanded the associations (ἑταίρα/*collegium*) which had been reintroduced by Gaius', he also forbade the Jewish synagogue meetings in the same legislation, although he allowed their other religious practices to continue.[23] Like Augustus, his legal perception of the Jewish community was that it was an association that had to be restrained.[24]

While there is no extant evidence of Nero's specific policy on associations in Rome, in the Roman colony of Pompeii 'illegal associations in the town were dissolved'. So legal procedures for authorisation and cancellation were still in place is his Principate.[25] Imperial policy was consistent with the perception that associations were hotbeds of sedition and therefore needed imperial and senatorial investigation into their activities. The parameters that Augustus stipulated were applied in subsequent Principates.

It is being suggested that, in the minds of Roman officialdom, a Christian community would have been looked upon no differently

---

[21] O.F. Robinson, *The Criminal Law of Ancient Rome*, 80.

[22] Philo, *Flaccus* 4, 'The associations (ἑταιρείας) and clubs (συνόδους), which were constantly holding feasts under pretext of sacrifice in which drunkenness vented itself in political intrigue, he dissolved and dealt sternly with the refractory.'

[23] *OGIS* 57.3.1. A cognate of the term ἑταῖρος was also used of members of religious groups and of Jews in a Cilician inscription. According to Dio his reason for not rejecting Jews from Rome at the beginning of his reign was that 'it would have been hard without raising a tumult', Dio Cassius 60.6.6.

[24] P. Richardson, 'Early Synagogues as *collegia* in the Diaspora and Palestine', ch. 6, has convincingly argued that in the Diaspora synagogues operated as associations.

[25] Tacitus, *Annals* 14.17. The circumstance that gave rise to this was a major incident in the theatre at a gladiatorial spectacular and the Senate report on it that followed.

from the Jewish community, that is, as an association. In Rome the church comprised Jewish converts, including a number named in Romans 16.[26] The noted Roman jurist and governor of Achaea, Gallio, declared the Christian community in Corinth to be a Jewish group involved in ideological wranglings that were outside his remit (Acts 18:15).[27]

The Augustan procedures for the regulation of associations in Rome were still in force, because Claudius banned again those formerly disbanded in the Principate of Augustus. The Christian community, gathering as a separate entity from the Jewish synagogues in Rome, would have been an unauthorised and therefore an illegal 'association' as there is no evidence that it had sought or secured imperial and then senatorial approval. It would have had to demonstrate that it was not political, but was engaged in that which benefited the public good. If, by the time of Nero, the term *Christiani* was used of Christians in Rome, this would have confirmed that those who gathered could possibly be involved in some illegal or clandestine activity. Therefore, it would have been open to the suspicion of political activity.[28]

How did Christians define themselves for the outsider? While care needs to be exercised in reading later centuries back into the first, the self-description of what Tertullian at the end of the second century called 'the business of the Christian club' (*factio*) may provide some clues:

> We are an association (*corpus*) bound together by our religious profession, by the unity of our way of life and the bond of our common hope ... We meet together as an assembly and as a society ... We pray for the emperors ... We gather together to read our sacred writing ... With the holy words we nourish our faith ... After the gathering is over the Christians go out as though they had come from a 'school of virtue'.

He was adamant 'it should not be called a political club but a council'. As Wilken notes, this chapter is full of technical terms used

---

[26] On Rom. 16 see A.D. Clarke's discussion in chapter 4 of this volume.

[27] See my 'Gallio's Ruling on the Legal Status of Early Christianity', 213–24.

[28] Suetonius uses the term of them in Nero's Principate, *Nero* 16.

in relation to associations.[29] Tertullian clearly found it a helpful analogy to use the phenomenon of the activities of an association to explain to his audience who did not understand the activities of the Christian community. He insisted, however, that the church was not an association.[30] In the apostolic period, did the Roman Christians define their community in terms of a legal entity, that is, as an association, or as a community operating according to the norms of an association? Of the Roman Christian community no evidence of its self-definition from this period survives.

Paul did not define them as an association nor teach them to emulate the ways in which they functioned; rather he formulated much of the life of the Christian community over against it. Roman Christians were the 'vessels of mercy', both Jews and Gentiles, according to Paul, and as such 'the people of God'. He did not use the term one might expect had the concept been borrowed from Greek or Roman, *politeia*, namely δῆμος, but λαός. It would be clear to them that this designation was not made on his own apostolic warrant, but on the basis of a prophecy from the Old Testament – 'As indeed he says in Hosea' in Romans 9:24–6, quoting from the prophet (Hos. 2:23). That text was the grounds for Gentile Christians, along with the Jewish members of their community, bearing the title 'the people of God', to which Paul added 'sons of the living God' completing the citation.

In chapters 12–15 Roman cultural norms confront God's will for individual Christians who must no longer define themselves as 'a Roman citizen' ('Ρωμαιότης/*civis Romanus*), 'a foreigner' (ξένος/*alienigenus*) or even 'a cosmopolitan' (κοσμοπολίτης) of a worldwide empire, but as sons and daughters of God. That called for a major reorientation in thinking and behaving. It is spelt out primarily as the antithesis to the culturally shaped norms of associations in Rome as the following sections on the important spheres of life germane to Christian existence will show.

---

[29] R.L. Wilken, *The Christians as the Romans Saw Them*, 46.

[30] *Apology* 39. See Philo's comparable approach, paralleled with the Therapeutai and the sophists. For Philo's discussion of associations see T. Seland, 'Philo and the Clubs and Associations of Alexandria', ch. 7; and on the former matter my *Philo and Paul Among the Sophists of Alexandria and Corinth*, 62–6.

The Privileged and One's *Persona* (12:3–21)

One's legal *persona* (πρόσωπον) determined one's place and privileges in society. The conventions governing social interactions were determined by 'good status' (εὐπρόσωπον).[31] Rome had long defined its citizens and strangers by rank and status with senators, *equites, plebs,* including freedmen, as well as foreigners, and encouraged the former groups by means of privileges to be proud of who they were.[32]

The senators were the highest class and were social equals of the emperor, who in the Julio–Claudian dynasty liked to portray himself as one of them, distinguished only by the fact that he was 'the first citizen', hence the reference to their Principates from the time of Augustus onwards. While he effectively usurped the traditional powers of the Republican Senate, he did much to define the boundaries of its members both by way of privilege and of moral restraints. The wearing of the broad purple stripe on the tunic (*latus clavus*) and other senatorial privileges were extended to all close relatives and descendants of a senator to the third generation. In the time of Tiberius it was extended to those he wished to promote regardless of family origins.

Augustus also sought to curb the excesses of this class with sumptuary laws on expenditure on banquets, clothes and jewellery and forbade members from appearing on stage. He penalised young men from the elite class who would not marry and sought to restrict those whom they could marry. Additional benefits were granted to those with three children. This was social engineering on an unprecedented scale but, at the same time, had the calculated effect of highlighting class distinctions.

Membership of *equites Romani* had long required a property qualification and Augustus distinguished them more markedly from the senatorial class by establishing a financial differential. The former group was expanded with additional jurors who acquired the right to wear the special gold ring of senators and *equites* and to

---

[31] For an examination of the use of this term and the stem πρόσωπον, see my *Seek the Welfare of the City*, 137–9.

[32] For a helpful summary see M. Goodman, 'The City of Rome', ch. 17.

sit in the front rows of the theatre. It was from this class that the senatorial ranks were filled.

Even the Plebs were divided into two groups so that the privilege of the corn dole was granted to those who were 'official' Plebs of Rome. Free corn was not for the sustenance of the very poor or the non-official Plebs, but rather for those of moderate means whose position in society was defined by this privilege, the origins of which stretched back into the Republican period. According to Augustus there were a little more than 200,000 official Plebs who qualified for this benefaction. This number appears to have increased under Nero.[33]

Those who secured manumission after a period of bonded service in Roman households were granted freedmen status along with Roman citizenship. Their links to the emperor were further secured by providing them with the opportunity to become priests of the imperial cult of Augustus. They therefore had not only the privileges of Roman citizenship, but also some form of religious connection with the emperor. In some cases freedmen were known to have amassed huge fortunes and under imperial patronage might rise to positions of influence in the empire.[34]

Then there were the vast number of foreigners who came to Rome from all over the empire. Their reasons for settling in Rome were either for political advancement or financial advantage. Noy's magisterial work based primarily on the vast amount of epigraphic material in Rome gives some indication of how both Roman citizens from the provinces, and provincials were attracted to, and functioned in, the capital.[35]

Status in Rome was clearly seen in two important areas of social life. In the time to Augustus under the *lex Julia theatricalis* seating in the theatres was assigned according to social rank, so that all would be well aware of their place within society.[36] As theatregoing was extremely popular with all classes in Rome and

[33] G. Rickman, *The Corn Supply of Ancient Rome*; and P. Garnsey, *Famine and the Food Supply in the Graeco-Roman World*, 223–36.

[34] On the priests of Augustus see D. Fishwick, *The Imperial Cult in the Latin West*, 2.1:609–16.

[35] Noy, *Foreigners at Rome*.

[36] E. Rawson, *'Discrimina ordinum'*, 83–114.

through New Comedy had a moulding influence on social mores, legislation such as that of Augustus only heightened class consciousness in public contexts.[37]

The distinctions of class were also consciously reflected in conventions that were observed at public as well as private dinners. At public banquets the person of highest rank took his portion of food first and the remainder took theirs in descending order. Pliny wrote to commend an aspiring provincial administrator: 'I mean to congratulate you on the way in which you preserve the distinctions of class and rank [at a dinner]; once these are thrown into confusion and destroyed, nothing is more unequal than the resulting "equality".'[38] Private dinners also operated on the grounds of social hierarchy where the quantity served and the quality of it, as well as the seating arrangements, were all used to draw attention to social status.[39]

It is significant that Paul's first call to understand the will of God over against conforming to this age touched the very heart of Roman society, i.e., how one should reflect on oneself. God's will is explicated in the following sentence with 'I say' (λέγω) placed at the beginning for emphasis: 'For I say through the grace of God given me to all among you (παντι τῷ ὄντι ἐν ὑμῖν) not to think of himself [or herself] more highly (ὑπερφρονεῖν) than what it is necessary to think (παρ' ὃ δεῖ φρονεῖν), but to think for the purpose of exercising a sober judgement (ἀλλὰ φρονεῖν εἰς τὸ σωφρονεῖν) according to the measure of faith that God has assigned each' (12:3). Here Paul is making a fundamentally anti-cultural call. It includes 'all' in the community, and involves an assessment not derived from membership of any social classes, but an understanding of what Paul calls 'the measure of faith' assigned by God to each. It was not bestowed on the basis of class or education, but by the will of God and was for the benefit of all (12:3). That gift would deliberately blur all social distinctions

---

[37] T. Crisafulli, 'Representations of the Feminine', 222–3.

[38] Pliny the Younger, *Letters* 9.5.3.

[39] J.H. D'Arms, *Commerce and Social Standing in Ancient Rome*. On equal and unequal private dinners in relation to the Lord's Supper see my ' "Private" Dinners and Christian Divisiveness (1 Corinthians 11:17–34)', in my *After Paul Left Corinth*, ch. 7.

because that which assigned places in Roman culture was no longer relevant in the Christian community.[40]

Paul explicated this revolutionary way of self-definition further in the following sentences by way of an analogy. He likened the group not to a legal or social entity, but to a body composed of many parts, that is, 'many limbs', which all have different functions. These gifts presumably were a synonym for 'the measure of faith'. They had been assigned by God to individuals according to the grace given and not on the basis of ethnicity or social privilege. The terms are functional just as parts of the body are (12:4–5). The call was not defined educationally, but functionally with the use of the gifts of prophecy, service, teaching, exhortation, giving, leading and acts of mercy (12:6–8). While social class constituted the very fabric of Roman society and defined one's place in it, Paul undercut that with his call to re-evaluate self-understanding, not in terms of privilege, but in terms of the roles that God, and not society, had assigned. Paul thereby overthrew centuries of Roman self-definition based on class with this counter-cultural self-evaluation based on God-given gifts that were meant to benefit others or contribute to their needs.

Roman class distinctions bred strife and jealousy both between and within different classes. Private conflicts spilt over into the arena of *politeia* and resulted in vexatious litigation, which was played out in the civil courts and was a powerful aspect of life in Rome endorsed by Roman law. The stated offence was simply the excuse for legal action, but the reason was the public humiliation of one's opponents.[41] Romans dreaded such action being mounted against them, knowing that the judge and the jury were required to pronounce judgement on the basis of the rank and status of the plaintiff and the accused. They were aware that the verdict could create a new set of inimical relationships and that it was not the awarding of damages, but the public shame that most hurt the one

---

[40] E.A. Judge, 'Cultural Conformity and Innovations', 24, who sees this section as 'an attempt to formulate a new principle of social relationships'.

[41] D.F. Epstein, *Personal Enmity in Roman Politics 218–43 BC*; and for evidence from the Roman empire see my 'Civil Law and Christian Litigiousness 1 Corinthians 6:1–8', in my *After Paul Left Corinth*, ch. 4.

against whom the judgement went.[42] Judges and juries in civil litigation were corrupt in their judgements and Roman law provided a legal context to be vindictive and to secure revenge.[43]

Dionysius of Halicarnassus in his history of the Roman people best sums up what was seen as a high-minded response in Rome: 'We love those who do us good and hate those who do us harm, and renounce our friends when they injure us, which is just, honourable and holy.'[44] Enmity was a key issue at the centre of much activity in Roman society. In stark contrast Paul instructs the Christian community how to seek the resolution of conflict and how to handle their adversaries (12:9–13).

The will of God for his people was blessing rather cursing – the latter being resorted to as a central endeavour in much Roman religious activity (12:14).[45] Empathy and harmony rather than haughtiness and snobbishness were to be the hallmarks of their relationships (12:15–17). Retaliation was proscribed and actions that commended themselves to all were to be the concern of Christians (12:17). The pursuit of peace was the call of God, aware of course that peace would not always be secured (12:18). Vengeance, however much it was justified in Rome, was categorically proscribed, for divine judgement would run its course. Paul's justification for not pursuing redress through the normal legal channels available to those with social status in Rome were two citations from the Old Testament, namely Leviticus 19:18 and Deuteronomy 32:35. Conciliatory gestures of meeting the real needs of enemies, such as hunger and thirst, and non-retaliation would ultimately bring about repentance, citing Proverbs 25:21–2. Evil must not be victor, but good must win the day (2:21). Romans 12:14–21 certainly provided a counter-cultural response to the lack of harmony and the undercurrent of strife and jealousy that pervaded relationships in Roman society.

---

[42] R.A. Kaster, 'The Shame of the Romans', 1–19.

[43] 'Civil Law and Christian Litigiousness', 60–4.

[44] *Roman Antiquities* 34.1–2. See D.L. Balch, 'Political Friendship in the Historian Dionysius of Halicarnassus, *Roman Antiquities*', ch. 6, for an extensive discussion of case studies based on relating to the handling of enemies and enmity relationships.

[45] For the background see my 'Religious Curses and Christian Vindictiveness', in my *After Paul Left Corinth*, 166–9.

The legal endorsement of class distinctions in entertainment both in public and in private and the outworking of enmity relationships in Roman law were established mores against which Paul spelt out in Romans 12 the will of God for his people.

The Privileged and *Politeia* (13:1–7)

The term *politeia* (πολιτεία) traditionally described those activities that occurred outside one's household, and covered areas broader than political institutions in the Roman empire.[46] However, in this passage Paul refers to two specific activities of one aspect of *politiea* – the judicial arm that operated the courts and acquitted or punished breaches of the law, and the binding obligation on the 'Council and the People' to honour civic benefactors publicly in an appropriate way. Paul's teaching on this part of *politeia* was in the context of these dual roles of government. Naturally he used the traditional categories of the first century to describe these aspects of *politeia*, which had a long history in Greek and Hellenistic culture as well as in that of Rome, hence the dichotomy (13:3).[47]

While the administration of justice needs no further explanation, the command 'to do good' and the obligation of the authorities for 'praising those who do good' in this context needs clarification. That the reference could be to moral good has to be ruled out, given that the sure promise of the ruling authority to praise such good is guaranteed in a city estimated to have housed over one million inhabitants[48] – 'do good and you [singular] *will* have praise from the authority' (ἀγαθὸν ποίει, καὶ ἕξεις ἔπαινον ἐξ αὐτῆς), (13:3b). Paul knew that there were individuals in the Christian community of sufficient influence and financial means to undertake such benefactions, some of whom he named in Romans 16.

---

[46] J. Bordes, *Politeia dans la pensée greque jusq' à Aristote*, 116ff.

[47] See my *Seek the Welfare of the City*, 34.

[48] The population of Rome in the early empire is estimated to have been somewhere between 440,000 and 1,000,000, with the lesser figure being favoured in more recent studies; see Noy, *Foreigners at Rome*, 15–22.

The officials who ruled a city were traditionally required to praise or honour formally those who gave some form of civic benefaction to the city. There are two reasons for arguing that here Paul was endorsing the civic benefaction tradition. First, he defined the dual role of governing authorities using this dichotomy. The praising of those who did good was clearly understood in Greek and Roman society, both in that time and in previous centuries, to be the public honouring of civic benefactors.

Second, epigraphic evidence from large numbers of benefaction inscriptions uses the verb to 'praise' and its cognate noun. In Greek inscriptions the honours were traditionally spelt out in the resolution of the city authorities in the section beginning with 'it has been decreed' (δεδόχθαι). The authority commenced the final clause with either ἵνα or ὅπως in keeping with the benefaction genre. That was designed to inform all who read it that the city knew how to award with appropriate honour those who were, and by implication might become, its benefactors. Here, as in a parallel passage in 1 Peter 2:14–15, the injunction to do public good is a Christian responsibility and it expected public recognition. Paul endorses the long-established custom of civic benefactions for individual Christians in the community where the person would be 'praised', that is, publicly honoured as 'good and noble' (καλὸς καὶ ἀγαθός) in the civic sense of the word. This was a synonymous phrase for 'benefactor' as attested by epigraphic evidence.[49]

First Peter 2:14–15 declares this to be an appropriate way to counter those who made accusations against Christians as evildoers, for benefactors had the confidence of 'the Council and the People'. Unlike that letter, Romans is here discussing the issue of the governing authorities of Rome in a tranquil era, and hence the added reason to silence false accusations was not needed.

---

[49] For an extended discussion of this see my 'Civic Honours for Christian Benefactors: Romans 13:3–4 and 1 Peter 2:14–15', in my *Seek the Welfare of the City*, ch. 2. For benefaction inscriptions in Rome itself see *IGRR* et al. A.D. Clarke, 'The Good and the Just in Romans 5:7', 138–40, produces evidence from literary and epigraphic evidence that the 'good' man in the context of Rom. 5:7 is not 'a friend' but one's benefactor.

Did Paul have in mind that, by undertaking this form of public service, one of the stipulations of Augustus concerning non-political groups was met?

Paul further outlined the will of God in terms of the two forms of obligation. He prescribed the payment of 'all one's dues' that a person living in Rome owed to the authorities. He used the term 'obligation' (ὀφειλή), which meant either a financial or social debt (13:7). They are discussed here as 'tangible' and 'intangible' obligations, the first being 'tribute' (φόρος) and 'taxes' (τέλος), and the second 'reverence' (φόβος) and 'honour' (τιμή).

The first two are not the same, as Strabo demonstrates in relation to different revenues derived from people either by way of tribute and tax.[50] The former is a levy placed on people and land, while the latter is a levy on income, goods and services. The former was levied on everyone living in the empire, apart from those Roman citizens living in Roman colonies that enjoyed the *ius Italicum*. Those who were not Roman citizens living in Rome had to pay tribute as well. How did one escape what was known as the 'provincial' tax? 'I went into service to please myself, and preferred being a Roman citizen to going on paying taxes as a provincial.'[51] While this was a great source of revenue for the imperial authorities it was not welcomed in the provinces. With great fanfare Nero announced his unexpected proposal to grant 'immunity from tribute' (ἀνεισφορία) to all the inhabitants of Greece on his visit to Corinth in AD 66. It was greeted with a huge outpouring of praise, although it was not to prove a permanent immunity.[52]

Paul gives reasons why Christians who are required to pay tribute are to do so: 'For because of this, [i.e. 'for conscience' sake because it is a legal requirement, 13:5 you are paying tribute', and 'for they are God's servants attending constantly to this very thing'. In giving this injunction Paul could be seeking to overcome any

---

[50] Strabo, *Geography* 2.5.8.

[51] See Petronius, *Satyricon* 57, where Hermeros defends himself at a dinner party in Rome from his move in selling himself into bonded household slavery in the home of a Roman citizen for a specified period and on securing manumission also obtained Roman citizenship. For a discussion of this procedure see my *Seek the Welfare of the City*, 154–9.

[52] *ILS* 8794.

reluctance to pay, or closing any loopholes that Christian Jews returning to Rome and others residing there who were not Roman citizens, might seek to use to avoid paying the provincial tax, that is, tribute. This reason may contrast in some way with that of Agrippa, king of Judaea who argued that Jews had to pay tribute in order to demonstrate to Rome that they were not insurrectionists.[53]

Taxes were levied on a great number of items sold in the city-controlled markets throughout the empire as well as in Rome. Professions and services also attracted such levies. They had long been an important source of revenue for any city, for the imperial authorities retained a grip on all indirect taxes levied on goods sold in the markets and on other commercial activities.[54] An important part of the duties of the prefect of the city was the supervision of those known as the 'tax-farmers' who were responsible for collecting indirect taxes.[55]

Paul also enumerated the intangible obligations of Christians: 'reverence' (φόβος) to whom reverence is due and 'honour' (τιμή) to whom honour is due (13:7b). Given that Christians were meant to respect the role of those who exercised justice (13:3), the first obligation could well refer to showing respect to the judicial authorities both in the criminal and civil courts of Rome.

The second term, 'honour' (τιμή), was used in a range of semantic domains within *politeia*. The requirement that authorities honour benefactors has already been noted, but, in this verse, the honouring is to be done by the Christian inhabitants of Rome. The reference is to rulers (οἱ ἄρχοντες) to whom due honour was to be paid. Paul naturally did not use the term 'reverence' (εὐσέβεια) with respect to the supreme authority in Rome who demanded that veneration traditionally given to gods.[56]

Searches have been made for the specific Roman *Sitz im Leben* of Romans 13:1–7. Friedrich, Pöhlmann and Stuhlmacher argued that the tax protests of AD 58 and the eviction of the Jews from Rome in 49 meant that Paul was keen that returning Jewish residents of Rome, such as Prisca and Aquila, did not draw

---

[53] Josephus, *Bellum Judaicum* 2.403–5.

[54] L. de Ligt, *Fairs and Markets in the Roman Empire*, 169.

[55] M. Goodman, *The Roman World 44 BC–AD 180*, 98.

[56] Fishwick, *The Imperial Cult in the Latin West*, vols. 1.1 – 2.1.

attention to themselves by not paying their taxes.[57] Strobel argued that in the time of Claudius there was widespread dissatisfaction over the granting to procurators of the right to levy taxes.[58] However, unlike Gaius who increased taxes, Claudius cancelled those imposed by his predecessor early in his Principate.[59] It was Nero who increased the level of taxes towards the end of his reign, introducing a new tax on tenants payable retrospectively for twelve months to the privy purse. He also required all classes in Rome to pay an income tax, evasion of which was a criminal offence.[60]

The last suggestion may best reflect the situation to which Paul was responding, especially if the privileged in Rome were no longer exempt from income tax. Christian attitudes towards authorities in Rome were not based on taking a low profile to confirm they were not insurrectionists. Popular antagonism against increased taxes did not cancel the tangible and intangible obligations of Christians towards the authorities. The community had to recognise that the authorities in Rome who acted as God's vicegerents in discharging their office were to be duly honoured and their laws observed. These obligations were the will of God, and not the general secular reactions in *politeia*.

The Privileged and Promiscuity (13:8–14)

Rome was known for its young party-going set. Romans 13:13 well describes the activities of those who have come 'of age', with the assuming in the forum of the male toga (τὸ ἀνδρεῖον ἱμάτιον) as Plutarch described the Roman *toga virilis*, this garment signifying entry into adulthood.[61] The first two doublets 'not in revelling and drunkenness' (κώμοις καὶ μέθαις), and 'not in debauchery and licentiousness or lewdness' (κοίταις καὶ ἀσελγείαις), epitomised

---

[57] Tacitus, *Annals* 13.50; Suetonius, *Nero* 44.1–2. J. Friedrich, W. Pöhlmann and P. Stuhlmacher, 'Zur historischen Situation und Intention von Röm 13:1–7', 131–66, for discussion.

[58] A. Strobel, 'Furcht, wem Furcht gebührt: Zum profangriechischen Hindergrund von Rm. 13.7', 61–2.

[59] T.M. Coleman, 'Binding Obligations in Romans 13:7', 313.

[60] Suetonius, *Nero* 44.

[61] *Brutus* 14.4.

many of the activities of the privileged younger set in Roman society, especially as a summary of behaviour at Roman dinners.[62]

Rome was known for its taverns where 'revelling and drunkenness' was typical behaviour. The first two couplets, 'revelling and drunkenness' and 'debauchery and licentiousness', went hand in hand in what was commonly known as 'the after dinners'. At such a time in private feasts, tables were reserved for 'the drinking bouts which followed as part of, but not the only event in "the after-dinners", as they were commonly known'.[63] This refers to the activities of courtesans who entertained their partners sexually both during the dinner and afterwards while reclining on the dinner couches, if the pictorial representations of these events can be trusted.

Even the somewhat restrained Cicero wrote of young men after the receiving of their *toga virilis*:

> If there is anyone who thinks that youth should be forbidden affairs even with courtesans (*meretricii amores*), he is doubtless eminently austere, but his view is not only contrary to the licence of this age, but also to the custom and concessions of our ancestors. For when was this not a common practice? When was it blamed? When was it forbidden? When, in fact, was it, that 'what is allowed' was not allowed?[64]

Such promiscuous activities, not contrary to 'the licence of the age' (*saeculi licentia*), were often carried forward into marriage where it was no longer a case of fornication, but of adultery. Aulus Gellius recorded the Republican attitude that left the husband, but not his wife, free to commit adultery: 'It is also written, regarding the right to kill; "If you catch your wife in adultery, you can kill her with impunity; she, however, cannot dare to lay a finger on you if you commit adultery, *nor is it the law*." '[65] Augustus

---

[62] E. Eyben, *Restless Youth in Ancient Rome*, for a full discussion of this topic; and also on promiscuity in Rome see R.A. Pitcher, 'Martial and Roman Sexuality', 1:309–15.

[63] Philo of Alexandria, *Vita* 54.

[64] Cicero, *Caelius* 20.48.

[65] *Attic Nights* 10.23. He 'copied Cato's words from a speech called *On the dowry*, in which it is stated that husbands who caught wives in adultery could kill them. "The husband," he says, "who divorces his wife is her judge, as though he were a censor." '

introduced legislation that made a wife's adultery a criminal offence punishable by relegation once she was divorced. The man could still commit adultery with courtesans at banquets or in other liaisons and do so with impunity in Roman society as an acceptable Roman social custom. It was still not 'the law'. While the new Roman woman emerged and challenged this and other inequalities, she still stood culpable for her adultery if her husband divorced her and instituted criminal proceedings.[66] The absence in the law of any proscription of a man's adultery, except in cases of incest and then with an important caveat,[67] meant that his privileged position was protected.

Two observations should be made about the terminology of Romans 13:13. The reason for being more specific about the *Sitz im Leben* is that Paul does not use his normal terms for 'fornicators' and 'adulterers' (πόρνοι and μοιχοί, 1 Cor. 6:9) when he proscribes sexual conduct in this verse. It is not simply misconduct in 'private' he is dealing with.

Second, one of the unique features of Latin sexual terminology is that Roman society borrowed Greek terms and transliterated them for sexual activities of which they did not approve. As Adams notes, 'Forms of perversion [to the Roman mind] … tend to be ascribed particularly to foreign people, and those perversions may be described by a word from the foreign language in question. Various words to do with homosexuality in Latin are of Greek origin (*pedico, pathicus, cinaedus, catamitus*; *cf. malacus* [μαλικός].'[68] It is significant that none of the terms in 13:13 were derived from the semantic field of sexuality found in Latin as Greek loan words. Therefore we can assume that Paul is describing here sexual activities of which Roman society approved.

---

[66] See my *The New Roman Woman and the Pauline Churches* for discussion of this movement and the legislation of Augustus against them.

[67] For evidence of this see my *After Paul Left Corinth*, 45–7.

[68] J.N. Adams, *Latin Sexual Vocabulary*, 228. It was a criminal offence to penetrate a Roman male citizen sexually, although not so if the passive partner were a foreigner, hence the borrowing of the last term in 1 Cor. 6:9 and the discussion 'Roman Homosexual Activity and the Elite (1 Cor. 6:9)', in my *After Paul Left Corinth*, 110–20. Of the ongoing application of the *lex Scantinia* see 111–13.

Paul's third doublet 'not in strife and jealousy' (ἔριδι καὶ ζήλῳ) are words that were used in a number of semantic fields including education and associations as well as politics, in fact, wherever Romans operated in social situations. Athenaeus noted of the after-dinner conduct that 'after drinking comes mockery, after mockery filthy insults, after insults a law-suit, after the lawsuit a verdict'.[69] It is possible that Paul is referring to a particular *Sitz im Leben*. All these activities are described as 'the flesh' (13:14).

The proscriptions in 13:13–14 are set within two important contexts. The first is the intention of the Mosaic Law concerning relationships, where love towards one's neighbour is seen as its fulfilment (vv. 8–10). Paul deliberately framed his summary of the law with the command not to be under obligation for anything, except to love one another, explaining that the one who loves his neighbour fulfils the law (13:8). Binding obligations, often financial, towards committed relationships, including family, masters and patrons, formed the fabric of Roman society. The obligation to love, let alone love an immediate neighbour or those within proximity, must have struck a highly unfamiliar note in the mind of any inhabitant of Rome who heard it for the first time.

Second, 13:11–12 challenges another accepted norm in Roman society, namely its philosophical assumption of the eternity of the world and, by deduction, Rome as 'the eternal city'. Furthermore, the replication of an ordered cosmos in town planning with its centuriation pattern, its symmetrical architecture, the carving of aspects of the natural world into the ceilings of its magnificent buildings, and its precision in the layout of its gardens, all re-enforced an orderly, eternal world.[70] In addition to the commandment to love,

---

[69] *Deipnosophists* 2.36.

[70] Suetonius, *Augustus* 28: Augustus said, 'I found Rome built of sun-dried bricks; I leave her clothed in marble' and not only with respect to the constitution but beyond that he wanted to die knowing that 'these foundations will abide secure'. On the relationship between the nature of things and architecture see Vitruvius, *Architecture* 9, 'Preface' 17–18, and his reference to Lucretius, *The Nature of Things*. On the eternity of the world and architectural replication see my discussion in 'The Seasons of this Life and Eschatology in 1 Corinthians 7:29–31', 324–7, and literature cited.

Paul gave a wake-up call to the Roman community when he refers to a culturally foreign, but eschatological reality for the Christian. He emphatically stated, 'And knowing this, "the hour" (καὶ τοῦτο εἰδότες τὸν καιρόν), that it is high time for you to wake up from sleep' (13:11). The reason is that the consummation of their salvation was now closer than when they first believed, and the dawn was about to break. The deeds of the night would not stand the scrutiny of stark daylight, and therefore they must put on the armour of light and operate appropriately, he argues.

In a society where relationships were conducted on the basis of filial, patronal or financial obligations, Paul's thrust in this segment of ethical instruction – not to be under obligation for anything, but to love your neighbour – must have sounded totally counter-cultural to Roman ears. Within the framework of the intention of the law of Moses, bolstered by the eschatological reality, Paul demanded that Christians abandon unbecoming conduct, even though Rome endorsed such unbridled hedonism as part of 'the licence of the age', where 'what is allowed' there was not 'allowed' among Christians because it was not the will of God.

The Privileged and the Powerless (14–15)

The internal situation that Christians in Rome faced was a difficult one because clearly there were different opinions on fundamental matters of fellowship. To eat meat or not to eat it, may seem of little consequence in the twenty-first century where vegetarianism has become an acceptable alternative. There Christians were willing to live with the differences of conviction, but both sides had become involved in arguments. By the time Paul wrote they were in a 'stand-off' position passing judgement on each other, the stronger Christian despising 'the weak'.

What circumstances gave rise to the non-meat-eating group? Meat was a commodity that, like other foodstuffs, was sold through the official markets of any city, including Rome, and was subject to indirect tax. Josephus records an important official resolution in Sardis for the restoration of Jewish rights in concert with what Rome had done in restoring to the Jews 'their laws and freedom'. In meeting its obligations to the Jewish inhabitants, the city agreed to provide kosher food for sale through the officials who oversaw the market. It was simply following the lead of 'the Roman Senate and People' in the restoration of these privileges.[71] Food declared to be 'suitable' was sold in the official markets in Rome.[72] The Jews had been punished in Rome and elsewhere by having their rights and privileges cancelled, one of which was the provision of kosher food.[73]

When Claudius banned the Jews from Rome in AD 49 the officials who controlled the meat market would have withdrawn the provision of 'suitable food'. There may have been some in Rome who were no longer eating meat because kosher meat was not available in the markets. Given the official control of the market it would have required the action of a senior official, with the emperor himself giving his approval, for the reopening of the segment of the market for the Jews. Historically that had been the case both in Sardis and Rome in the Republican period and as Claudius had relegated the Jews from Rome, so the restoration of the privilege would require Nero's approval. This could explain the reason why some returning Jews who were Christians refused to eat meat that had been offered to idols in keeping with the slaughtering tradition in Graeco-Roman cities of the first century. At some stage in Rome there needed to be the official restoration of the Jewish privilege. There are good reasons for suggesting this *Sitz im Leben* gave rise to the problem.

An even more fundamental issue divided Christian opinion. A dispute had arisen over the appropriate day to observe, and therefore to gather together, as Christians. Some argued that there was only one day that was appropriate, their contention being supported by the creation ordinance for a sabbath and the long Jewish tradition as to the day on which it was observed. In addition,

---

[71] *Antiquitates Judaicae* 14.261.

[72] On markets generally see De Ligt, *Fairs and Markets in the Roman Empire*.

[73] ἐπιτήδεια = 'suitable', i.e., kosher. When Josephus wrote from Rome at the end of the first century he included in Bk 14 copies of decrees still extant in the capitol according to the introduction to ch. 10. For a discussion see M. Pucci Ben Zeev, *Jewish Rights in the Roman World*, 381–408.

they could point to the legal situation in Rome concerning that tradition. Augustus had respected the *mos maiorum* of the Jews and therefore conceded both their weekly sabbath and permission for official *plebs* who were Jews to secure their corn dole at another time, if the appointed day fell on their sabbath.[74]

Others in the community took a completely different view – that observation of days and food was a matter of spiritual indifference. However, they did not intend to concede any ground to the Jewish Christian sabbath-keepers; they were not merely judging them, but openly deriding them for their ill-conceived convictions. Paul wished to stifle individual criticisms and asked, 'Why do you [singular] pass judgement on your brother?' and, even more telling, 'Why do you [singular] despise your brother?' (14:10).

If it was possible to determine the actual *Sitz im Leben* it would go some way to understanding the seemingly unusual implications of the Pauline statements made in these chapters. It has been assumed that in the vast population of Rome's urban sprawl there was but one single Christian meeting. That assumption has been challenged.[75] It could have been the case in 14–15:21 that Paul was seeking to provide a way forward that would facilitate Christian gatherings coming together as one. Some form of 'negotiations' may already have commenced among the Christians in Rome, but a total impasse had been reached on two critical issues discussed in chapters 14–15. Paul's former co-workers in Corinth and Ephesus, Prisca and Aquila, may have been informally enlisted to act as private mediators. This role was not unknown in Rome, and in the provinces there were those who sought the help of former governors and provincial officials who had returned to Rome for a variety of reasons.[76] In this case the appeal was made from Rome to Paul in Corinth to provide some mediation by letter to everyone.

---

[74] Robinson, *The Criminal Law of Ancient Rome*, 80.

[75] E.A. Judge and G.S.R. Thomas, 'The Origins of the Church at Rome', 81–94.

[76] R.P. Saller, *Personal Patronage under the Early Empire*, 169, 175ff. For approaches to provincials with influence to mediate see, for example, Junia Theodora from first-century Corinth, R.A. Kearsley, 'Women in Public Life in the Roman East', 203–8, for the text.

If there was one congregational meeting in Rome – it is that meeting in the home of Prisca and Aquila to which Paul would later send his greetings (16:4–5) – then a split would be imminent. Seeking a person outside the community who would be acceptable to both sides to broker a deal would be an acceptable Roman solution. On the other hand there may have been an informal approach to Paul who would have been someone acceptable to both Jews and Christians, given his role as apostle to the Gentiles. The latter is the subject on which he, in effect, closed this discussion. He reminded the church of the grace of God given to him to be 'a minister of Christ to the Gentiles … to win obedience from the Gentiles [who] have come to share in their [the Jews] spiritual blessings' (15:16, 18, 27). He was concerned that the work of God was in danger of being destroyed, so the latter reconstruction might be more credible.

Whatever the *Sitz im Leben*, these chapters represent his move to break what must have seemed to the Christians in Rome two intractable problems that either blocked a move to come together or prevented them splitting asunder. Does the way Paul discussed the matter support both or either of these reconstructions?

It is clear from the text that those who were regarded as 'weak' in the faith were immediately challenged by the meat-eating and non-sabbatarian Christians (14:1). Paul's first requirement was that they must be received, but not for the purpose of engaging in polemical discussion of these issues. His subsequent argument was that both sides had to agree to differ, but not to judge, and especially not to denigrate the 'weak'. Paul called an immediate halt to judging, because it was not the place of either group to do so. That prerogative belonged solely to the Lord and it was therefore totally inappropriate for either group to stand in judgement. Furthermore, the kingdom was not about food and drink, but about 'righteousness and peace and joy in the Holy Spirit' (14:17). Paul was convinced that although they held different opinions on these issues and would continue to do so, they must stand together.

Paul made three demands on the Christians in Rome. The first is that 'we were not to judge (κρίνωμεν) one another', but to 'decide this rather (ἀλλὰ τοῦτο κρίνατε μᾶλλον)' – never to put a stumbling block or hindrance in the way of a brother (14:13). The force of this demand is reflected in the use of the strong adversative and the placing of the neuter demonstrative pronoun before the verb.

The second is introduced by 'so then' (ἄρα οὖν), which Paul used to sum up the argument of the previous paragraph: 'So then they must pursue what makes for peace and mutual upbuilding' in contrast to denigration (14:19).[77] The work of God could be destroyed for the sake of food, for it was wrong to make others stumble over this issue (14:19).

Paul's third requirement is totally unexpected. The 'strong', whose theological position Paul actually supported, were told that 'they were under an obligation' not to please themselves on these issues, but to bear with the infirmities of the 'weak'. An obligation in Roman society bound the one who owed it to fulfil it. It was the strongest requirement that could be laid on the conscience of another.[78] It is also interesting to note that here Paul identified with the strong by stating 'we who are strong' and 'each one of us' (15:1).

However, the 'strong' had no right to demand their own way on these critical issues for the community: 'for Christ did not please himself, but as it is written, "The reproaches of those who re-proached you fell on me."' A further reason is given for this injunc-tion to the strong in Rome – 'For whatever was written in former days was written for our instruction, that by steadfastness and by the encouragement of the scriptures we might have hope.' On the basis of this Paul asked that God would grant 'them to operate in such harmony with one another' (τὸ αὐτὸ φρονεῖν ἐν ἀλλήλοις κατὰ Χριστὸν Ἰησοῦν) – 'in order that (ἵνα) you may with *one voice* glorify the God and Father of our Lord Jesus Christ' (15:6). 'There-fore' (διό) to do this, they had to welcome one another in the same way that Christ received them – to the glory of God (15:7). Paul cites one of three Old Testament passages which requires Gentile Christians to praise the Lord with their Jewish brothers: 'Rejoice,

---

[77] M. Thrall, *Greek Particles in the New Testament*, 10–11, on the use of this combination of particles in Paul to summarise the preceding discussion.

[78] For a full treatment of the Roman laws of obligation and their outworking in Romans 14–15 see J.D. Duncan, 'Obligation as a Means of Conflict Resolution in Romans 14:1–15:7', and on the former issue his chapter 'The Roman Law of Obligations and its Bias toward the Strong', ch. 3.

O Gentiles, with his people' – Psalm 18:49 cited in 15:9.

What were the practical implications of the injunctions in 15:1–7? The strong had 'to bear with' (Βαστάζειν) the weak on the two issues discussed in chapter 14. There would be one weekly 'holy' day and no meat in fellowship situations. How else could they glorify God with one voice if there was no consensus as to the day on which they were to meet (15:6)? Would it be possible to welcome or receive one another in any Christian table fellowship if the 'strong' insisted on serving meat (15:7)? The gathering for table fellowship would have to take into account the sensitivity of the 'weak' in the same way that Paul had required the Corinthians to do at a private dinner (1 Cor. 10:27–9). In Roman Corinth, for the sake of the conscience of the person who indicated that the meat had been offered to idols, one did not eat it. While in Rome the setting was not explicitly Jewish, the same principle would apply. Furthermore, the serving of meat to some and not to others would replicate the dinner conventions that consciously re-enforced class and hierarchical distinctions (see p. 78). This would be highly inappropriate in the Christian gathering.

The 'strong', therefore, had to concede these two issues to the 'weak' for the sake of unity. Paul, who was quite open with the community concerning the consequences, demanded this. They, like Jesus, would be reproached by outsiders who could identify them because they followed Jewish practices. That identification was made subsequently in the last period of Nero's Principate when the blame for the fire of Rome was passed on to the Christians who could be readily identified in Rome.

Not only did Paul demand that the strong must not seek their own way, but both the presence and absence of certain key terms in chapters 14–15 indicates why that would be inappropriate. From the perspective of an association one could expect that the term 'member' would be used, but it is missing. This occurs in the funeral association of Diana and Antinous where all the stipulations were addressed to 'members', that is, not the limbs of a body, but part of an association.[79]

He refers to Phoebe as a patron of his apostolic mission and

---

[79] *ILS* 7212 (AD 133).

commends her to the Christian community in Rome in connection with a forthcoming visit (16:2).[80] Yet any invoking of specific client/patron language and the implication that the patron in his position of strength determined the course of action on the part of the 'weak' to the 'strong' in chapters 12–15 is missing. In a stunning reversal of cultural norms, the 'strong' have obligations to the 'weak' based, in part, on the overarching mercies of God and more closely tied to the *imitatio Christi* in terms of the theologically correct who could not get their own way on these issues (12:1; 15:1–2). Client/patron language was expunged from Paul's mind as he discussed this issue.

Attempts to cast the discussion of these chapters in the light of respect and benefactions of friends are also unconvincing. Saller has pointed out that 'In contrast to the words *patronus* and *cliens*, the language of *amicitiae* [friendship] was sufficiently ambiguous to encompass both social equals and unequals. This ambiguity was exploited and there was a tendency to call men *amici* rather than *clientes* as a mark of consideration.' However he goes on to note that this did not have the effect of creating egalitarianism in Roman society because 'a new grade in the hierarchy was added as relationships with lesser *amici* were labelled *amicitiae inferiores* or *amicitiae minores*'.[81] Sevenster noted the absence of the word 'friend' in chapters 12 – 15. He felt that it was highly significant that Paul avoided the use of terms such as 'friend' (φίλος) and 'friendship' (φιλία) and this stood out in comparison with Seneca. Judge also argued that Paul avoided the status implications of a patronal friendship.[82] Yet Mitchell and Fiore have argued that the concept of ancient friendship provides important arguments and vocabulary for Paul in this passage.[83]

Plutarch, the late first-century and early second-century AD philosopher, discussed both the real and the ideal: 'Most friendships are actually shadows, imitations, and images of that first friendship

---

[80] D. de Silva, *Honor, Patronage, Kinship and Purity*, does not discuss Phoebe's role as patroness in relation to Paul.

[81] Saller, *Personal Patronage*, 11.

[82] J.N. Sevenster, *Paul and Seneca*, 174–80; and E.A. Judge, 'Paul as Radical Critic', 196.

[83] A.C. Mitchell, ' "Greet the friends by name" ', 232.

which Nature has implanted in children toward parents and in brothers toward brothers.' Plutarch knew in practice that friendship 'cannot be concerned with the relationship between persons of different social levels'. O'Neil has concluded on reading 'How to Tell a Flatterer from a Friend' and 'On Having Many Friends' Plutarch's belief that one cannot have many real friends: many friends equal many flatterers. In the composite volume *Greco-Roman Perspectives on Friendship* to which O'Neil and Mitchell both contributed, the former's observations seem not to have incorporated allusions to Paul's letters into the quest for friendship. Mitchell himself acknowledges the 'conspicuous sacristy of the words φιλία and φίλος', citing the conclusion of both Klauck and Judge that this avoidance was deliberate.[84] Mitchell believes that 'Paul's emphasis on mutual esteem and benevolence, the pragmatic end of community and equality [in 14:1–15:13], looks a lot like the object of friendship in the Classical tradition'.[85] However, the 'politics of friendship' is absent from Paul's discussion of these issues, as is the very term itself.[86]

In this section the term 'household servant' with God as the master (14:4) is used by way of an analogy in the call to cease the inappropriate judging of another; 'brother' is the other designation with an unusual concentration of references (14:10, 13, 15, 21).[87] The term 'brethren' or 'brothers or sisters' may sometimes be used in contemporary Christianity either with the defining phrase 'in Christ' implied or explicitly stated in certain traditions. This would have startled the inhabitants of Rome because the unqualified sibling relationship Paul claimed in these chapters is with the

---

[84] *Moralia* 479C–D. E.N. O'Neil, 'Plutarch on Friendship', 107, 110.

[85] Mitchell, ' "Greet the friends by name" ', 232, citing B. Fiore, 'Friendship in the Exhortation of Romans 15:14–33', Proceedings of the Eastern Lakes and Midwest Biblical Societies 7 (1987), 99.

[86] B. Rawson, *The Politics of Friendship*.

[87] It does occur elsewhere in 1:13. 7:1, 4, 8:12, 29, 10:1, 11:25, 12:1, 15: 14, 30, and 16:17 in the plural to address the whole community. It is used once in 9:3 where it is explicated by the term 'my kinsmen by race' and in 16:14 where the Christians who were with five named individuals are greeted; cf. 9:29, and in the following verse 'the saints' is used as an alternative designation. The only other letter where the term is invoked at critical stages of Paul's arguments is in 1 Corinthians.

majority of those whom he had not met. They were not natural or adopted members of a particular family. Roman law zealously guarded close kinship relations and many resisted Augustus's attempts to intrude into that realm with criminal law.[88] It was certainly not a descriptive term that anyone would ever have expected to find in a group in the area of *politeia* in Roman society, even in a religious association in the Julio–Claudian era.

How was this term used in the argument? It occurs in 14:10 in relation to passing judgement and actually despising 'your brother', that is, members of your own family, and presumably holding them and their views to ridicule. The command is 'therefore' never to pass judgement on one another and to resolve never to stumble or hinder a brother (14:13). Actions must not injure a brother by what you eat, even though, like Paul, you are persuaded in the Lord Jesus that there is nothing unclean. To do so is to walk no longer in love in relationship to others in this particular family (14:15). That point is reiterated in relation to meat and wine or anything that causes a 'brother' to stumble (14:21). A powerful faction in the Christian community could win the day in the heart of the empire with a culturally endorsed response, but it would be catastrophic for the future with the work of God (14:20). Paul's counter-cultural call to the 'family' was obviously a very critical one.

In this section I am not suggesting that there were not those in the Christian community in Rome who may have felt that membership of an association, patron/client conventions or those of inferior friendships could provide something of a useful paradigm for relationships in the uncharted waters of their new community. Paul's discussion, however, reflects a fundamentally different construct that flies in the face of all these precedents in Roman society. He requires the Roman community to relate to one another in terms of sibling relationships and therefore equals. The 'family' was to care for one another, respect each other's views and bear with the weaker brothers. This was something distinctly foreign to the spirit of the age of the Julio–Claudians who under-stood themselves as either members, clients or friends in relation to others.

---

[88] For discussions see my *After Paul Left Corinth*, 125–6.

Conclusions

Trajan ended his response to Pliny's correspondence with a ruling that proscribed the governor from initiating criminal prosecution against Christians whose names were listed on anonymous pamphlets. He argued that this would create a bad legal precedent in Bithynia, adding that such a move was 'not in keeping with the spirit of our age' (*nec nostri saeculi est*).[89] On the other hand Paul, in discussing the above issues (Rom. 12–15), was also concerned lest the conduct of the Roman community should become conformed to 'the spirit of our age'.[90]

In terms of privilege Paul was a critic of the self-reflecting nature of Roman society in terms of social status. He proposed a radically new way of operating with self-understanding determined by the gifts God assigned to individuals and which were given to be used for the service of others. He refuted the fractious nature of the Roman upper social classes with their acceptance of enmity and revenge through the courts.

On the important matter of Roman Christians and *politeia* in relation to civic authorities, civic obligations, criminal actions and civic benefactions, Paul required the observing of tangible and intangible obligations. Any widespread resentment of taxation in Nero's Principate provided no exception for the Christian community.

Paul's concern was that Christians should 'put on the Lord Jesus' and make no provision for the flesh to indulge in activities not just tolerated, but endorsed by, Roman society. In this he ran counter to the spirit of the age, for he did not endorse the view that one 'cannot dare to lay a finger on you [a male]' if you engaged in promiscuous activities.

Paul's view was radical – although divided on significant issues, the Christian community had to stand together, which ran counter to the way in which disagreements in Roman society were

---

[89] Pliny the Younger, *Letters* 97.

[90] T. Rajak and D. Noy, '*Archisynagogos*', 75–93, draw attention to the fact that the Jewish Diaspora synagogue had been much influenced by the spirit of the age in *politeia* in the early empire. They show for example how its *archisynagogos* had been cast in the role of patron and philanthropist.

resolved. He 'plunders the Egyptians' at this point, taking hold of the Roman concept of obligation, and forbade the strong to please themselves on issues not central to the kingdom, thus overthrowing the Roman view that 'might is right'.

The above investigation draws attention to the fact that ethical instructions in the New Testament were often set over against the norms endorsed by society. As an apostle to the Gentiles Paul's instructions in all but civic benefactions undermined many of the foundations of Roman culture. In Romans 12–15 he should not be regarded as either a social conservative or a social realist, but as a radical critic of the prevailing culture of privilege in Rome's society, underpinned, as it was, by Roman law.

Bibliography

Adams, J.N., *Latin Sexual Vocabulary* (London: Duckworth, 1982)

Balch, D.L., 'Political Friendship in the Historian Dionysius of Halicarnassus, *Roman Antiquities*', in Fitzgerald, *Greco-Roman Perspectives on Friendship*, ch. 6

Ben Zeev, M. Pucci, *Jewish Rights in the Roman World: The Greek and Roman Documents Quoted by Josephus* (Tübingen: J.C.B. Mohr, 1999)

Bordes, J., *Politeia dans la pensée greque jusq' à Aristote* (Paris: 'Les Belles Lettres', 1982)

Bruce, F.F., *The Acts of the Apostles: Greek Text with Introduction and Commentary* (Grand Rapids: Eerdmans / Leicester: IVP, 1990[3])

Clarke, A.D., 'The Good and the Just in Romans 5:7', *TynBul* 41.1 (1990), 138–40

Coleman, T.M., 'Binding Obligations in Romans 13:7: A Semantic Field and Social Context', *TynBul* 48.2 (1997), 307–27

Crisafulli, T., 'Representations of the Feminine: The Prostitute in Roman Comedy', in T.W. Hillard et al. (eds.), *The Ancient Near East, Greece and Rome* (Ancient History in a Modern University; Grand Rapids: Eerdmans, 1998), 222–3

Crook, J.A., *Roman Life and Law, 90 BC–AD 212* (New York: Cornell University Press, 1967)

D'Arms, J.H., *Commerce and Social Standing in Ancient Rome* (Cambridge, MA: Harvard University Press, 1984)

Duncan, J.D., 'Obligation as a Means of Conflict Resolution in Romans 14:1 – 15:7' (PhD diss. forthcoming)

Epstein, D.F., *Personal Enmity in Roman Politics 218–43 BC* (London: Croom Helm, 1987)

Eyben, E., *Restless Youth in Ancient Rome* (London: Routledge, 1993)

Fishwick, D., *The Imperial Cult in the Latin West: Studies in the Ruler Cult of the Western Provinces of the Roman Empire*, 2 vols. (Leiden: E.J. Brill, 1987–93)

Fitzgerald, J.T. (ed.), *Greco-Roman Perspectives on Friendship* (Atlanta: Scholars Press, 1997)

Friedrich, J., W. Pöhlmann and P. Stulmacher, 'Zur historischen Situation und Intention von Röm 13:1-7', *ZTK* 73 (1976), 131–66

Garnsey, P., *Social Status and Legal Privilege in the Roman Empire* (Oxford: Clarendon Press, 1970)

—, *Famine and the Food Supply in the Graeco-Roman World: Responses to Risks and Crisis* (Cambridge: Cambridge University Press, 1988)

Goodman, M., 'The City of Rome: Social Organization', in idem (ed.), *The Roman World 44 BC–AD 180* (London: Routledge, 1997), ch. 17

Hargis, J.W., *Against the Christians: The Rise of Early Anti-Christian Polemic* (New York: P. Lang, 1999)

Hillard, T.W., et al. (eds.), *The Ancient Near East, Greece and Rome* (Ancient History in a Modern University; Grand Rapids: Eerdmans, 1998)

Judge E.A., and G.S.R. Thomas, 'The Origins of the Church at Rome: A New Solution', *RTR* 25 (1966), 81–94

—, 'Cultural Conformity and Innovations', *TynBul* 35 (1984), 1–24

—, 'Judaism and the Rise of Christianity: A Roman Perspective', *Australian Journal of Jewish Studies* 7.2 (1993), 82–98, republished *TynBul* 45.2 (1994), 355–68

Kaster, R.A., 'The Shame of the Romans', *TAPA* 127 (1997), 1–19

Kearsley, R.A., 'Women in Public Life in the Roman East: Iunia Theodora, Claudia Metrodora and Phoebe, Benefactress of Paul', *TynBul* 50.2 (1999), 203–8

Kloppenborg, J.S., '*Collegia* and *Thiasoi*: Issues in Function, Taxonomy and Membership', in Kloppenborg and Wilson, *Voluntary Associations in the Graeco-Roman World*, ch. 2

Kloppenborg, J.S., and S.G. Wilson (eds.), *Voluntary Associations in the Graeco-Roman World* (London: Routledge, 1996)

Ligt, L. de, *Fairs and Markets in the Roman Empire: Economic and Social Aspects of Periodic Trade in a Pre-industrial Society* (Amsterdam: J.C. Gieben, 1993)

Mitchell, A.C., ' "Greet the friends by name": New Testament Evidence for the Greco-Roman *topos* on Friendship', in Fitzgerald, *Greco-Roman Perspectives on Friendship*, 225–62

Noy, D., *Foreigners at Rome: Citizens and Strangers* (London: Duckworth with the Classical Press of Wales, 2000)

O'Neil, E.N., 'Plutarch on Friendship', in Fitzgerald, *Greco-Roman Perspectives on Friendship*, 105–22

Pitcher, R.A., 'Martial and Roman Sexuality', in Hillard et al., *The Ancient Near East, Greece and Rome*, 1:309–15

Pöhlmann, Friedrich, W., and P. Stuhlmacher, 'Zur historischen Situation und Intention von Röm 13:1–7', *ZTK* 73 (1976), 131–66

Rajak, T., and D. Noy, '*Archisynagogos*: Office, Social Status in the Graeco-Roman World' *JRS* 83 (1993), 75–93

Rawson, B., *The Politics of Friendship: Pompey and Cicero* (Sydney: Sydney University Press, 1978)

Rawson, E., '*Discrimina ordinum*: the *lex Julia theatricalis*', *PBSR* (1987), 83–114

Richardson, P., 'Early Synagogues as *collegia* in the Diaspora and Palestine', in Kloppenborg and Wilson, *Voluntary Associations in the Graeco-Roman World*, ch. 6

Rickman, G., *The Corn Supply of Ancient Rome* (Oxford: Clarendon Press, 1980)

Robinson, O.F., *The Criminal Law of Ancient Rome* (London: Duckworth, 1995)

Saller, R.P., *Personal Patronage under the Early Empire* (Cambridge: Cambridge University Press, 1982)

Seland, T., 'Philo and the Clubs and Associations of Alexandria', *Voluntary Associations in the Graeco-Roman World*, ch. 7

Sevenster, J.N., *Paul and Seneca* (Leiden: E.J. Brill, 1961)

Sherwin-White, A.N., *Roman Society and Roman Law in the New Testament* (Oxford: Clarendon Press, 1963)

Silva, D. de, *Honor, Patronage, Kinship and Purity: Unlocking New Testament Culture* (Downers Grove: IVP, 2000)

Strobel, A., 'Furcht, wem Furcht gebührt: Zum profangriechischen Hindergrund von Rm. 13.7', *ZNW* 55 (1964), 61–2

Thrall, M., *Greek Particles in the New Testament* (Leiden: E.J. Brill, 1962)

Van Nijf, O.M., *The Civic World of Professional Associations in the Roman East* (Amsterdam: J.C. Gieben, 1997)

Wilken, R.L., *The Christians as the Romans Saw Them* (New Haven: Yale University Press, 1984)

Winter, Bruce W., *Seek the Welfare of the City: Early Christians as Benefactors and Citizens* (Grand Rapids: Eerdmans / Carlisle: Paternoster Press, 1994)

—, 'The Seasons of this Life and Eschatology in 1 Corinthians 7:29–31', in K.E. Brower and M.W. Elliott (eds.), *Eschatology in Bible and Theology: Evangelical Essays at the Dawn of a New Millennium* (Downers Grove: IVP, 1997), 324–7

—, 'St. Paul as a Critic of Roman Slavery in 1 Corinthians 7:21–23', Proceedings of the International Conference on St. Paul and European Civilization, *Paúvleia* 3 (1998), 339–54

—, 'Gallio's Ruling on the Legal Status of Early Christianity' *TynBul* 50.2 (1999), 213–24

—, *After Paul Left Corinth: The Influence of Secular Ethics and Social Change* (Grand Rapids: Eerdmans, 2001)

—, *Philo and Paul Among the Sophists of Alexandria and Corinth* (Grand Rapids: Eerdmans, 2001²)

—, The New Roman Woman and the Pauline Churches (Grand Rapids: Eerdmans, forthcoming)

4

Jew and Greek, Slave and Free, Male and Female: Paul's Theology of Ethnic, Social and Gender Inclusiveness in Romans 16

Andrew D. Clarke

Summary

Paul's programmatic statement in Galatians 3:28 that in Christ there is neither Jew nor Greek, slave nor free, male nor female, is reflected also in the encouragement and commendation given without discrimination to both Jew and Greek, slave and free, male and female in his greetings to the church in Rome. Paul's theology regarding the inclusion of the Gentiles within the church of Christ, spelled out in the earlier chapters of the epistle, is powerfully reinforced by both his ethical instructions and his references to specific individuals in the later chapters. Similarly, his positive highlighting of the labours of both women and those from slave stock fosters that sense of inclusiveness that Paul argues ought to characterise the church of Christ. In this chapter I shall examine Romans 16 for evidence of the outworking of Paul's stance on social inclusion across ethnic, social and gender barriers.

Introduction

From the time of the early patristic writers onwards, scholarly interaction with the weighty theological chapters of Romans 1 – 11 has predictably eclipsed the more ephemeral material in

Romans 16.[1] Similarly, the paraenetic chapters of Romans 12 – 15 receive significantly greater attention among scholars than the greetings and final remarks of Paul in his closing chapter. Such apostolic 'trivia' as are found in Romans 16, while they provide a fascinating window on the social situations to which and from which Paul was writing, are so specific to their original contexts that they offer little that is of direct relevance to congregations in different locations or later periods. Furthermore, they contribute little to Paul's preceding arguments, which, after all, form the nub of the apostle's communication to the Christians in Rome.

In recent decades it has been more widely recognised that each of the books and letters of the New Testament presupposes an original social situation. Careful sociological and rhetorical analysis of these texts frequently enables us to understand more about the social situation of either the original recipient(s) or sender(s), or both. This, in turn, can contribute to a more nuanced interpretation of the theology of the writer(s).[2] If a similar approach is taken regarding even Paul's closing remarks in Romans 16, it may be that we shall understand something more, not just about those first Christians in Rome (and in Corinth) who are there mentioned by name, but also about the writer himself. In the following, an attempt will be made to review the prosopographical material in Romans 16 that may in turn reveal something about Paul's own understanding of the nature of the Christian community.

Notwithstanding the comparative paucity of scholarly, secondary literature on Romans 16, a number of works offer significant insight into this area. Peter Lampe's extensive monograph, first published in 1987, and expanded in a second edition two years later, remains the principal study of the social location of the Christians in the early Roman congregations.[3] Lampe has helpfully presented some of this

---

[1] The extant works of Irenaeus, Cyprian and Tertullian do not refer to Romans 15 or 16 at all.

[2] Cf., with regard to Romans 16, R.E. Oster, ' "Congregations of the Gentiles" (Rom 16:4)', 39, who writes, 'the theology and ethical injunctions that characterise this Pauline letter are a direct and concrete response to circumstantial and local issues of Christianity occurring in the mid-first century in Rome'.

[3] P. Lampe, *Die stadtrömischen Christen in den ersten beiden Jahrhunderten*.

material in other articles,[4] and an English translation of the earlier monograph has been announced.[5] The work of this scholar has rightly been recognised for its monumental significance. In addition to these Lampe works, some chapters in Karl Donfried and Peter Richardson's collection *Judaism and Christianity in First-Century Rome* helpfully consider the social location of the Roman Christians.[6]

The Integrity of Romans

A study of the historical setting of Romans 16 raises questions about the authenticity of this final chapter of Paul's letter. The Pauline authorship of Romans has received little challenge. The length of the letter, namely whether it originally included chapters 15 and 16, and the destination of the final chapter, however, have been repeatedly disputed from various quarters over the past 250 years.

Three elements of evidence contribute to this puzzle: the presence of what appears to be a concluding blessing in Romans 15:33; the varied textual tradition that locates Romans 16 in different places; and the number of individuals listed in the closing remarks of the letter, together with the extraordinary familiarity Paul appears to have with them. How could there be such familiarity if Paul had not at this stage visited the city? One explanation widely accepted is that this final chapter originally had a different audience in mind, possibly Ephesus where he had indeed spent a considerable period of time. Accordingly, Romans 16 might have been, as it were, either a 'covering' letter that accompanied a copy of Romans for the benefit of a second congregation, namely at Ephesus, or a letter of recommendation commending Phoebe of Cenchreae to another congregation (Rom. 16:1–2).

---

[4] P. Lampe, 'The Roman Christians of Romans 16', 216–30; cf. also a number of Lampe's articles in the *ABD* focusing on named individuals.

[5] P. Lampe, *From Paul to Valentinus*.

[6] K.P. Donfried and P. Richardson (eds.), *Judaism and Christianity in First-Century Rome*. A recent doctoral dissertation, R.C.N. Holzapfel, 'Roman Christianity', also considers this material, but adds little of significance.

Lampe argues that for Paul to have a passing knowledge of some twenty-six Christians in the Roman capital is not a cause for surprise. The amount of travelling undertaken by people in the first century poses the possibility that Paul may have met some of these individuals in other locations. We know this to have been the case in particular with Aquila and Prisca who had earlier moved from Rome to Corinth, where they had spent time with Paul. It is clear from both Lukan and Pauline sources that for some time they were resident in Ephesus, from which city Paul wrote to the Corinthians, conveying greetings from this much-travelled couple (1 Cor. 16:19; Acts 18:19). Indeed, it may be that Aquila and Prisca were the source of Paul's knowledge of some of the figures mentioned in Romans 16 about whom Paul does not expand in detail.[7] By the time Paul writes to the Romans, it may be that these two leading figures in Christian mission have returned to Rome after the tension that led to the Claudian expulsion of the Jews in AD 49 had died down.

Furthermore, it may be noted that whether the destination was originally Rome or Ephesus, the list of names in Romans 16 draws attention to a significantly mobile group of individuals: Epaenetus (Rom. 16:5) was the first convert in Asia; Andronicus and Junia/Junias (Rom. 16:7) had been in prison with Paul, elsewhere than in Rome, and as those who were apostles before Paul, they probably lived at some time in Samaria or Judaea;[8] Aquila (Rom. 16:3) originally hailed from Pontus (Acts 18:2); and Phoebe (Rom. 16:1) was associated with the Achaian seaport of Cenchreae, near Corinth. Peter Lampe further suggests that the affection with which Paul refers to Ampliatus, Stachys and Persis (Rom. 16:8, 9, 12) might suggest that they were personally known to him other than in Rome; and similarly the significant citation given to Apelles as one 'tested and approved in Christ' (Rom. 16:10, NIV) might also suggest personal acquaintance.[9] Additionally, Peter Lampe has analysed the available epigraphic evidence from Rome and calculated the frequency with which those names in Romans

---

[7] E.g. Asyncritus, Phlegon, Hermes, Patrobas, Hermas, Philologus, Julia, Nereus and Olympas; so suggests, P. Lampe, 'Roman Christians', 220.

[8] J. Thorley, 'Junia, a Woman Apostle', 18.

[9] Lampe, *Die stadtrömischen Christen*, 138.

16 also appear in the Roman inscriptions. On the basis of these calculations he concludes that a number of the names are quite rare in Rome, and this *may* suggest that Apelles, Philologus, Stachys, Phlegon, Persis, Hermas, Asyncritus, Olympas, Patrobas and Herodion *may* have been immigrants.[10] This mobility, certain in the case of some, and conjectured in the case of others, strengthens the possibility that Rome may have been the original destination of this chapter.

It is significant that the textual tradition of the letter presents both a fourteen-chapter version and a longer version. The longer version, however, always finds Romans 15 and 16 together, although the doxology of Romans 16:25–7 is placed at the end of chapter 15 in the oldest witness, $\mathfrak{p}^{46}$. A significant study by Harry Gamble of the textual history of Romans has succeeded in persuading Joseph Fitzmyer against his previously held view, and the weight of scholarly opinion now favours a Roman destination for these closing comments as being at least as plausible as an Ephesian destination.[11]

A working assumption that Romans 16 was originally intended for a Roman audience will be adopted here, although my underlying thesis is more concerned with the Pauline authorship of these verses than their destination. In the light of this, we can now seek to assess Paul's stance regarding the social distinctives of ethnic origin, social status and gender roles in that congregation.

Ethnic Origin, Social Status and Gender Roles

The case for including Gentiles within the ancient Abrahamic covenant is the focus of much of Paul's discussion in Romans 1 – 11. In the final chapter of the letter there is little evidence from the onomastic data alone to establish the ratio of Jews to Gentiles in the Roman congregations. It will be argued, however, that there is

---

[10] Ibid. 140.
[11] H. Gamble, *The Textual History of the Letter to the Romans*; and J.A. Fitzmyer, *Romans*. Cf. also K.P. Donfried, 'A Short Note on Romans 16', 44–52. Note, however, the contrary view supported in N.R. Petersen, 'On the Ending(s) to Paul's Letter to Rome', 337–47.

evidence to support the view that there was ethnic diversity within the Christian community.

The last decades of the twentieth century have witnessed a heightened interest in the social location of the Pauline communities. To what extent did these congregations include a social mix? To what extent was social diversity the grounds for community unrest, even division? It will be argued that within Romans 16 itself there is also evidence of social diversity.

Those few scholars who have analysed the prosopographical material in Romans 16 have devoted most attention to the place of women within the Roman Christian community. Such a focus is prompted by the number and roles of women mentioned by Paul in this chapter. In the light of this, it will also be argued that the notable mix of men and women in Romans 16 is significant.

By considering in this way the ethnic, social and gender registers of those in the community who are mentioned in Romans 16, it will also, however, be possible to detect something about Paul's own stance on these distinctives. It will be appreciated that, in accordance with his own ethnic and social background as both a proud, male Jew and a Roman citizen, it is predictable that Paul's predisposition would be to reinforce many of the ethnic, social and gender divisions in society. In notable contrast to this stance, however, it will be argued that his theology of inclusion is mirrored closely in his practice.

It will further be suggested that the comments in Romans 16 are not a manipulative mechanism of social engineering designed to redound to his own glory, but rather a genuine reflection of the outworking of the gospel prefigured in the Abrahamic covenant. Paul's own attitude and stance towards the Christian congregation located in the heart of the Roman empire derives from his understanding of the gospel that is for all nations. This is reflected also in similarly inclusive statements in other letters in the Pauline corpus (e.g. 1 Cor. 12:13; Col. 3:11; and Eph. 2:13–16).

Jew and Greek

Jewish congregations and Gentile congregations in Rome

Paul does not speak about a single congregation (ἐκκλησία) in Rome,[12] as he does when he refers to the Christians in the cities of Corinth (1 Cor. 1:2; 2 Cor. 1:1; Rom. 16:23),[13] Cenchreae (Rom. 16:1), Laodicea (Col. 4:16; cf. also Rev. 1:11; 3:14), and Thessalonica (1 Thess. 1:1; 2 Thess. 1:1). Indeed, Romans 16 suggests that Christians were regularly meeting in a number of different houses, in possible contrast to the situation in Corinth where, at least on occasion, the church was able to meet in a single location, the home of Gaius.[14] Either the significant number of Roman Christians distributed across such a large city, or Jewish/Gentile tensions, may have prompted the need for groups to meet in a number of locations across the city.[15]

In addition to the group of Christians who met in the house of Prisca and Aquila in Rome, it should be noted that groups of Christians are associated with Asyncritus, Phlegon, Hermes, Patrobas and Hermas (Rom. 16:14), and similarly with Philologus, Julia, Nereus and Olympas (Rom. 16:15).[16] Lampe recognises the possibility that, in time, a further location for a group meeting was provided by Paul's own house arrest in Rome (Acts 28:30–1).[17]

---

[12] Cf. Rom. 1:7, 'to all those in Rome' (πᾶσιν τοῖς οὖσιν ἐν Ῥώμῃ).

[13] Cf. also the church in Jerusalem, Acts 8:1; 11:22; and the church at Antioch, Acts 13:1.

[14] In Rome, the house of Aquila and Prisca (Rom. 16:7) is singled out as if it were one of a few. In Corinth the house of Gaius is such that it can offer accommodation to the whole community (Rom. 16:23).

[15] Note the suggestion that, as with the Jews, the Christians were focused in a particular locality: Lampe, 'Roman Christians', 229.

[16] Ibid. 230. See the argument below suggesting that groups did not meet in the houses of Aristobulus or Narcissus; Lampe appears to assume that these two groups may have met as distinct groups. The evidence does not necessitate this, and it may even suggest otherwise in that a location may not have been available to them, although Lampe does point out some instances where the slaves in a given household met to cultivate their own religion independent of the patron of the house.

[17] Ibid. 230.

The Christians in the imperial capital certainly met separately and in a number of different locations, but do these different groups presuppose congregations that were segregated along ethnic lines? It may be argued that Christianity in Rome originated among the Jews, as evidenced by the tensions among Jews that prompted the Claudian expulsion.[18] To these Jewish Christians were soon added a significant number of Gentiles, however. The letter appears to presuppose the presence of both; indeed, Jews and Gentiles are variously and separately addressed at different points.[19]

The contrast between so-called 'weak' and 'strong' Christians in Romans 14 – 15 has from the work of Origen onwards been widely cited as evidence that there are two distinct Christian groups in the city. One continued to adhere to the Mosaic regulations (this group was predominantly Jewish, but may also have included some Gentile proselytes), whereas another had distanced themselves from the constraints of such boundary markers (this group was predominantly Gentile, but may also have included some Jews).[20]

Romans 14 – 15, however, presupposes situations where Christians with differing stances regarding food and holy days are clearly in contact with each other – and appear to be infringing each others' liberties even as they eat and celebrate certain days together.[21] The contact between Christians of different persuasions is sufficient to cause tensions. We note Paul's desire to conciliate between these opposing stances. Specifically, the 'strong' Christian is to welcome the 'weak' Christian (Rom. 14:1). Paul urges that the individual's conscience is to be protected and that peace and mutual edification are to be pursued (Rom. 14:19). The action to be adopted is one of acceptance (Rom. 15:7) notwithstanding ethnic distinctives, and of denying one's own liberties out of deference for another's faith (Rom. 14:21).

---

[18] R. Brändle and E.W. Stegemann, 'The Formation of the First "Christian Congregations" in Rome', 126.

[19] Jews may be in mind in Rom. 2:17; 4:1; 7:1; Gentiles may be the focus of Rom. 1:5–6, 13; 11:13; 15:14–21.

[20] For a recent assessment of competing views, see M. Reasoner, *The Strong and the Weak*, 1–23.

[21] Brändle and Stegemann, 'Formation', 125.

In the absence of any discussion of mixed table fellowship or a plea for unity across different congregations, it could be argued that these congregations distributed across Rome included a Jewish and Gentile mix. Whereas Paul similarly speaks of strong and weak in 1 Corinthians 8 – 10, the tensions evident in the Corinthian congregation probably did not surface because of ethnic diversity, but rather because of socio-economic diversity.

When Paul refers to the 'churches of the nations/Gentiles (αἱ ἐκκλησίαι τῶν ἐθνῶν)' in Romans 16:4, Richard Oster argues that 'Paul is using this phrase to describe congregational religious *culture* more than congregational *racial* character'.[22] Similarly, Paul in 1 Corinthians 12:2 speaks of the Corinthian Christians as formerly 'nations/Gentiles' (τὰ ἔθνη). This expression thus describes not their race, but their paganness.[23] In the case of the Christians in Rome it should be argued that cultural tensions surfaced when ethnically diverse congregations met. Paul's response is not to ride roughshod over such distinctives, but to recognise cultural diversity within these groups. Oster may then be in part correct when he argues that 'while the Pauline letters reveal a man willing to discipline, to make dogmatic impositions, and to censure moral sins, there was no apostolic attempt to clone congregations when it came to issues of cultural expression among believers'.[24] Where differences exist on matters of conscience or disputable matters of cultural diversity, then Christians should accept each others' differences in Christ, just as Christ himself has accepted them (Rom. 14:1–3). The tone of Paul's exhortation here differs from the invective presented in Galatians, not because he has now calmed down following a poorly considered and overhasty outburst, but because the issues in Romans 14 – 15 differ from those of Galatians, and indeed differ also from the earlier chapters of Romans where pursuance of the law, in particular the issue of circumcision, was material. On matters of cultural and ethnic diversity, both Jew and Gentile are one in Christ and must live together in harmony and unity.

---

[22] Oster, 'Congregations', 40.
[23] Ibid. 42–3. Cf. also Eph. 2:11.
[24] Oster, 'Congregations', 52.

Paul's kinspeople in the Roman congregations

We know from Acts 18:2 that Aquila (and possibly also Prisca)[25] is a Jew, although in Romans 16:3 Paul finds no need to highlight their ethnic origin. As a Jew, Aquila, together with his wife, had been ejected from Rome in response to the Claudian edict of AD 49. In Romans 16 Paul identifies three individuals who are his kinspeople or relatives (συγγενεῖς) to whom he sends greetings in Rome (Andronicus, Junia/Junias and Herodion, Rom. 16:7, 11), and three individuals who are his kinsfolk (συγγενεῖς) who send their greetings from Corinth (Lucius, Jason and Sosipater, Rom. 16:21). Paul is here referring specifically to Christians who are fellow Jews with him. The remaining names of individuals in Rome that are cited in Romans 16 give no cause to suggest a Jewish nationality, although the remote possibility exists that the name Mary (Rom. 16:6) derives from the Semitic root *miryam*.[26] The alternative text 'Mariam' followed by 𝔭[46] and others may also suggest a Semitic origin.

It is only in Romans that we see Paul using this term συγγενεῖς. In addition to the three very specific instances of this term in Romans 16 mentioned above, Paul also uses the term in Romans 9:3, where he appeals, with some emotion, to those of his own race: 'I could wish that I myself were accursed and cut off from Christ for the sake of my brothers, my kinsmen by race (υπὲρ τῶν ἀδελφῶν μου τῶν συγγενῶν μου κατὰ σάρκα)'.[27]

The term συγγενεῖς can be used in a wide range of contexts. It can refer to those family connections where there is a common ancestry or descent, and as such may be translated 'relative'. Beyond the familial context it can be used also of those of the same tribe or race. It is in this latter sense that Paul uses the term. He speaks of those of his own Jewish race. God's plan of salvation has included the Gentiles on the same terms as the Jews; but it is important for the Gentiles to recognise that, in the process of doing so, God has

---

[25] Luke uses the diminutive expansion of the name, Priscilla.

[26] Lampe, *Die stadtrömischen Christen*, 146–7, considers this view but argues against it on probability, favouring that she was a freedwoman or a descendant of a freed slave of the *gens Maria*.

[27] Cf. a similar usage of συγγενεῖς in Josephus, *Antiquities* 1.276; 2.269, 278; 9.249; 11.341; 12.257, 338.

not rejected the Jews. Paul's own specific singling out of three individuals in the Roman congregations as fellow Jews is, thus, significant. Those in Rome who are Gentile Christians need to be reminded both of the boast Jews have (Rom. 2:17–20; 3:1–2) and of the priority Jews have in the proclamation of the gospel (Rom. 1:16; 2:9–10). Indeed, 'there is no difference between Jew and Gentile – the same Lord is Lord of all and richly blesses all who call on him' (Rom. 10:12). The Gentiles need to accommodate the Jews in the new church, just as the Jews have been required to accommodate the ingrafting of the Gentiles (Rom. 11:11–24).

The tenor of Paul's message in Romans confirms the view that the church was predominantly Gentile, although Jews were present in sufficient numbers that their cultural distinctives were an issue.[28] I have also argued that the names listed in Romans 16 suggest the possibility of a significant Gentile, immigrant population. Notwithstanding these cultural differences, all of the Christians in Rome are to accept each other as Christ is accepting of all. Paul seeks not to suppress or overlook cultural differences, then, but draws attention to the cultural diversity that does exist and seeks to broker unity across this diversity.

Slave and Free

In Galatians 3:28 Paul also presents the case that in Christ there is no difference between slave and free. Social diversity between the comparatively rich and the have-nots marred relationships within the church at Corinth, the Roman colony from which Paul is writing Romans 16. The onomastic evidence of Romans 16 also suggests social diversity with the presence of slaves, freed and free people in the Roman congregations.

Peter Lampe suggests that Nereus, Persis, Herodion, Tryphosa, Tryphaena and Ampliatus were probably slaves or freed(wo)men; Julia and Junia were either freedwomen or descendants of freed(wo)men;[29] and Maria was most likely a freedwoman or

---

[28] Lampe, 'The Roman Christians of Romans 16', cites the following passages: Rom. 1:5–6, 13–15; 11:13, 17–18, 24, 28, 30–1; 15:15–16, 18; 9:3ff.

[29] P. Lampe, 'Iunia/Iunias', 32–4.

descendant of a freed(wo)man.[30] Indeed, 'more than two thirds of
the people for whom we can make a probability statement have an
affinity to slave origins'.[31] We do need to note, however, that the
freed state of a person does not say anything about their present
socio-economic status. There is ample documented evidence of
some freed slaves achieving significant social status, not least in the
colony of Corinth.

The names Urbanus, Prisca, Aquila and Rufus, on the other
hand, do not suggest slave origins.[32] Urbanus, Prisca and Aquila are
cited as Paul's co-workers, and Lampe argues that it may be that
Paul is making a social statement here.[33] This is an unnecessary
inference, and Peter Lampe, in any case, argues in contrast to many
commentators, that Aquila and Prisca, as independent craftworkers,
may not have been as wealthy as is often assumed.[34]

The householders Aristobulus and Narcissus (Rom. 16:10b,
11b) may not themselves have been Christians, although there are
Christians who are members of these two households.[35] This is
deduced from the absence of a specific greeting to either of
these individuals. Paul talks not of οἱ ᾿Αριστοβούλου or οἱ
Ναρκίσσου but of οἱ ἐκ τῶν ᾿Αριστοβούλου and οἱ ἐκ τῶν
Ναρκίσσου. Furthermore, Paul finds it necessary to draw attention
to the fact that he is specifically addressing those from the household of Narcissus 'who are in the Lord' (Rom. 16:11). The deduction is then made that those who are mentioned are slaves or
freedmen or freedwomen of these households. Lampe further sur-
mises that Aristobulus was not native to Rome, but had moved
there together with his household. This is deduced from the relative
scarcity of epigraphic occurrences of this name in the Roman
non-literary sources.[36] This is supposition and there is no evidence
to further the suggestion put forward by Lampe that the Christian

---

[30] Lampe, 'Roman Christians', 228.

[31] Ibid.

[32] Ibid. 227.

[33] Ibid. 228.

[34] Lampe, *Die stadtrömischen Christen*, 158–64; contra, e.g., G. Theissen, *The Social Setting of Pauline Christianity*, 83–96.

[35] Lampe, *Die stadtrömischen Christen*, 136.

[36] Lampe, 'Roman Christians', 222.

members of Aristobulus's household were converted before they came to Rome.

The comments Paul makes concerning Phoebe are the fullest: 'I commend to you our sister Phoebe, a διάκονος of the church at Cenchreae, so that you may welcome her in the Lord as is fitting for the saints, and help her in whatever she may require from you, for she has been a προστάτις of many and of myself as well' (Rom. 16:1–2, NRSV [Gk. shown]).

Phoebe is not a pre-existing member of the Christian community to which Paul is writing. Accordingly, the apostle is seeking to establish a warm integration of this lady into the church in the city to which she has travelled. The significance of Phoebe to our present discussion lies both in her social status and her gender. In what sense was Phoebe a διάκονος of the church in Cenchreae and a προστάτις of many including Paul? Was Phoebe a servant, minister, deacon or deaconess? Was she a patroness, guardian or helper? Predictably scholarship is divided over those who take a more elevated view of Phoebe's position and status,[37] and those who take a lower view.[38]

It is important to note that Paul does not describe Phoebe as a deaconess. To date, we have no occurrence of the feminine form of this word before the third and fourth centuries, and, therefore, it may confidently be regarded as an anachronistic translation of διάκονος in this much earlier context.[39] The remaining options are that she was a servant, minister or deacon. There are extant inscriptions citing female διάκονοι of cultic organisations in the non-literary sources from Ephesus.[40] John Collins has argued that the term διάκονος often has the technical connotation of an intermediary or spokesman, and in these instances it does not carry a servile sense. I have argued elsewhere that this is unconvincing with regard to the use of the term in the Pauline corpus, and that a more menial connotation is fundamental to

---

[37] Recently C.F. Whelan, 'Amica Pauli', 67–85.

[38] K. Romaniuk, 'Was Phoebe in Romans 16,1 a Deaconess?' 132–4.

[39] Whelan, 'Amica Pauli', 68.

[40] *I. Eph.* VII, 1.3414, 3415 and 3418 – undated; see G.H.R. Horsley, *New Documents Illustrating Early Christianity*, 4:240–1.

Paul's understanding of ministry.[41] It is interesting to note an inscription from a much later period, the fourth century, that recognises a lady called Sophia. She is described as a 'second Phoebe' (presumably an allusion to Romans 16), as well as both a δούλη of Christ and a διάκονος.[42]

Προστάτις is the feminine form of προστάτης. The reading παραστάτις, 'helper', in some inferior manuscripts has nonetheless influenced translation of the more reliable text, προστάτις.[43] Although a *hapax legomenon* in the New Testament, the presence of female benefactors, described by this term, is present in epigraphic sources.[44] In 1985 Ros Kearsley published an article that considered a contemporary inscription from Corinth, the Roman colony close to its eastern seaport of Cenchreae, which honours a benefactress, named Junia Theodora, described by a cognate of the word προστάτις.[45] The value of this epigraphic material to our understanding of Phoebe's activity lies in its contemporaneity, its location, and its detailing, in part, of the nature of activity that warranted the description προστασία. Theodora is recognised by the federal assembly of the Lycians for her hospitality to Lycians travelling to Corinth, and her meeting of their needs, possibly commercial. The text also alludes to the elevated civic circles in which she had influence, and among which she was able to act on behalf of the Lycians.[46] Kearsley notes that among all the inscriptions recognising Theodora there is no reference to any influence or support of either a father or husband. One possible male relative is cited, but he

---

[41] Cf. J.N. Collins, *Diakonia*, and A.D. Clarke, *Serve the Community of the Church*, 233–45.

[42] See Horsley, *New Documents*, 4:239; M. Guarducci, *Epigrafia greca IV*, 445.

[43] MSS F and G, ninth century.

[44] See Horsley, *New Documents*, 4:239–44.

[45] R.A. Kearsley, 'Women in the World of the New Testament', 124–37. A revised version has been republished in idem, 'Women in Public Life in the Roman East', 189–211. See also further discussion in B.W. Winter, *After Paul Left Corinth*, 185–6, 199–203. The inscriptions in question are published in D.I. Pallas et al., 'Inscriptions lyciennes trouvées à Solômos près de Corinthe', 143.

[46] Kearsley, 'Women in Public Life', 194–5.

is indebted to Theodora and indeed models himself on her, rather than vice versa.[47] Having assessed the evidence for Theodora, Kearsley's conclusion regarding Phoebe is that 'there appears to be no reason on grounds of sex alone to deny her the role of the benefactor of Paul and the Christians living in Kenchreai'.[48]

If Phoebe was indeed an independent woman, then her status would appear to have been high. Is Phoebe being commended to this church (whether Ephesus or Rome) *because* of her socio-economic status, however?[49] She has proved useful in a different situation (Cenchreae), and Paul here makes the pragmatic hint that she could also be of use to the recipients of this letter. The importance of Phoebe to the Romans is further highlighted, then, by citing her at the top of his list. Such an interpretation would, however, be contradictory of the stance he adopts elsewhere, namely that no additional respect should be given to someone on the basis of their socio-economic status.[50] This would be a manipulative picture of Paul, who is using the economic status of one person to further his networking elsewhere.

In contrast, it is to be noted that Paul combines the terms διάκονος and προστάτις in his description of Phoebe. If I am correct that the sense of διάκονος is servile, then Paul is commending this woman, not because people should defer to her significant status, but because, notwithstanding her status, she has succeeded in using her wealth in the service of others.

Analysis of these names in Romans 16 suggests that there is a notable socio-economic cross-section. This cross-section is reflected also in the latter half of the chapter, which includes a list of individuals in Corinth from whom Paul sends greetings.[51] It is not the servile status of those from slave stock that is highlighted, but it

---

[47] Ibid. 196–7.

[48] Ibid. 202.

[49] Whelan, 'Amica Pauli', 84–5.

[50] Cf., e.g., my discussion regarding the immoral member of the Christian community referred to in 1 Cor. 5 in *Secular and Christian Leadership in Corinth*, 73–88.

[51] Cf., e.g., my discussion of Erastus in A.D. Clarke, 'Another Corinthian Erastus Inscription', 293–301; idem, *Secular and Christian Leadership in Corinth*, 46–56; and idem, *Serve the Community*, 175–6.

may well be the serving attitude of the one person of a significantly high social status which is mentioned. Paul integrates all of these and finds reason to commend individuals regardless of their social status.

Male and Female

In Romans 16 Paul cites the names of a number of women who were Christians in or travelling to Rome – Phoebe, Prisca, Mary, Tryphaena, Tryphosa, Persis, Julia and possibly Junia. In addition Paul refers, but not directly by name, to the sister of Nereus (Rom. 16:15) and the mother of Rufus (Rom. 16:13).

Phoebe has been discussed above and requires little further comment here. It should be noted in passing, however, that Paul is drawing attention here to the benefaction of a woman. This, as we have seen, is not unique in mid-first-century Corinth, but is in contrast to an apparent reluctance among many translators of the New Testament to concede the possibility of a female benefactor.[52]

Prisca is invariably mentioned by both Paul and Luke in connection with her husband, Aquila (Acts 18:2, 18, 26; Rom. 16:3; 1 Cor. 16:19; 2 Tim. 4:19). It is widely noted that Prisca's name normally, and perhaps significantly, precedes that of her husband, although it should not be ignored that both Luke and Paul do also cite the two names in the reverse order. It is sometimes argued that the predominant citation of Prisca before her husband suggests that Prisca held the dominant role either within the marriage or within the Christian communities. This may well be correct, but is not a necessary conclusion. The interchangeable order may reflect the no less significant social statement that Paul here recognises equally the contribution of both partners. If so, he would be making no distinction on the basis of gender.

The debate that surrounds Junia/Junias is whether the name suggests a woman (Junia) or a man (Junias – a shortened form of Junianus). The accusative form as it appears in Romans 16:7 could be either feminine ('Ιουνίαν) or masculine ('Ιουνιᾶν). Accentation enables us to distinguish between the two, but this is not available

---

[52] Note, e.g., the sense of 'helper' in NIV and RSV, but 'benefactor' in NRSV.

in the earliest texts (majuscules). The late second or early third century $\mathfrak{p}^{46}$ actually has a different name, **IOYΛIAN**. In the rather later minuscules there is textual support for both renderings, with the ninth-century minuscule 33 giving a clear acute accent on the iota, thus favouring the feminine form, 'Iουνίαν. The supposition that Paul was addressing a female apostle, Junia, dominated among the patristic exegetes[53] and the early translations (Old Latin, Vulgate, Sahidic and Bohairic).[54] This is further supported by the absence of any reference to a Junias in extant ancient literary and non-literary sources.[55] Notwithstanding the extent and weight of the support among the patristics and the early translations for a feminine form, the Nestle-Aland twenty-seventh edition still favours the masculine accentation.

There are some twenty-eight individuals addressed in Romans 16. Twenty-six of these individuals are mentioned by name. Eighteen of the individuals are men; eight are women. While the majority are men, it is clear that the women are more often commended for their Christian activity.[56] One verb is used exclusively of the women Mary, Tryphaena, Tryphosa and Persis – 'to labour' (κοπιάω; Rom. 16:6, 12). This verb is used elsewhere by Paul of himself (1 Cor. 15:10; 2 Cor. 6:5; 11:23, 27; Gal. 4:11; Phil. 2:16; Col. 1:29; 1 Thess. 2:9; 3:5; 2 Thess. 3:8); of himself and Apollos (1 Cor. 3:8); of the apostles in general (1 Cor. 4:12); of the household of Stephanas, including Fortunatus and Achaicus, and similar worthy, leading individuals (1 Cor. 16:16; 1 Thess. 5:12); indeed as a characteristic that ought to be reflected in all believers (1 Cor. 15:58; Eph. 4:28). The verb implies honourable toil for the sake of the gospel or the Christian community, and is clearly a commendation.[57]

---

[53] John Chrysostom, *Homilies on the Acts of the Apostles and the Epistle to the Romans*, specifically draws attention in the fourth century to his assumption that Junia is unusually a woman with a keen interest in learning (φιλοσοφία).

[54] Thorley, 'Junia', 20.

[55] B. Brooten, ' "Junia … Outstanding among the Apostles" (Romans 16:7)', 141–4.

[56] Lampe, *Die stadtrömischen Christen*, 136–7.

[57] See also the discussion in A.L. Chapple, 'Local Leadership in the Pauline Churches', 398–429.

The group of Christians associated with Asyncritus, Phlegon, Hermes, Patrobas and Hermas (Rom. 16:14) is described as 'brothers' (ἀδελφοί). It is not necessary, however, to argue that this was an exclusively male fraternity. By analogy with the group identified by Philologus, Julia, Nereus and his sister and Olympas 'and all the saints with them' (Rom. 16:15), which included at least two women, there is no syntactical reason to argue that the latter group was any different from the former.[58]

Paul uses the same or comparable terms to describe both men and women. Prisca, Aquila, Urbanus are all fellow workers (Rom. 16:3, 9). As we have seen, it may well be that Andronicus and Junia are also recognised equally by Paul as male and female apostles (Rom. 16:7).

It should be recognised that the significance of women varied within the range of cultures evident in the Graeco-Roman world. Roman culture, for the most part, had a more liberated view of the status and roles of women. Greek culture, in contrast, continued in the first century to have a more restricted view of women. The Roman woman could have a significant role not only within the confines of her household, but also in wider society. This was most notably the case where she was of independent financial means.[59] Significantly, however, women are rarely found to have a high profile in public affairs.[60] The home, however, was the context for meetings of Christians in Rome, and elsewhere.[61] In Roman households, therefore, it should not be considered unusual that Paul is drawing attention to the significant role of women in their own households. Authority in the public sphere may have been counter-cultural, but authority in the private sphere, in Roman contexts at least, was entirely conventional.[62]

---

[58] See n. 15.

[59] Phoebe of Cenchreae may be one such woman.

[60] W. Cotter, 'Women's Authority Roles in Paul's Churches', 367.

[61] Cf. the case of Prisca and Aquila in Ephesus (1 Cor. 16:19) and Rome (Rom. 16:5); of Asyncritus, Phlegon, Hermes, Patrobas, Hermas and others (Rom. 16:14), and Philologus, Julia, Nereus, Olympas and others (Rom. 16:15) in Rome; of Gaius (Rom. 16:23) and Stephanas (1 Cor. 16:15) in Corinth; and of Nympha in Laodicea (or Colossae) (Col. 4:15); and of Philemon, Apphia or Archippus in Colossae (Philem. 2).

[62] Cotter, 'Women's Authority Roles', 369.

Wendy Cotter also draws the conclusion that since the Christian ἐκκλησία had adopted the term of the public civic assembly to describe itself, then we do have here the counter-cultural practice of women having positions of authority.[63] But may this case be overstated? I have argued elsewhere that Paul specifically does not want the church to be modelled on the political and civic patterns either in Greek or Roman contexts.[64]

The impression that remains when reading through the named addressees in Romans 16, incidentally in contrast to the names of those individuals in Romans 16 who are sending greetings from Corinth, is that there is a significant number of both men and women who appear to be treated by Paul indiscriminately.

Ethnic, Social and Gender Inclusiveness in the Wider Pauline Corpus

The Roman destination of chapter 16 may still be considered by some to be questionable. If this issue becomes settled in favour of a different location, the case can still be made that Paul's theology is matched by his practice. We see, for example, a similar stance on ethnic origin, social status and gender roles with regard to other congregations with whom he corresponds.

With some force, Paul makes a case to the Galatians that Gentiles and Jews together are to be incorporated into God's people on the same basis of faith alone. Indeed, the segregation of the two over table fellowship is a denial of the work of Christ.[65] Paul's argument in Galatians 3 is that Gentiles are themselves related to Abraham's seed through Christ. This bond between Jews and Gentiles is further strengthened by Paul's repeated efforts to ensure that those in the Jerusalem church who face financial hardship are supported by the predominantly Gentile churches of Corinth and Macedonia

---

[63] Ibid. 370.

[64] Contra ibid. 370–2, cf. the argument developed in Clarke, *Serve the Community*.

[65] Gal. 2:11–16. The case is similarly made in Eph. 2:11–22 that the work of Christ has been to break down the dividing barriers between Jews and Gentiles.

(Rom. 15:25–31; 1 Cor. 16:1–3; 2 Cor. 8 – 9). For the one who was apostle both to the Jews and the Gentiles, ethnic origin provides no barrier to his ministry across these divisions.

The notorious divisions that existed in the early Corinthian community were roundly opposed by Paul. Much scholarship in recent decades has endorsed, in broad terms, the case made by Theissen that these tensions derived from socio-economic inequalities. In addition to Paul's firm opposition to these divisions, and his determination that the Corinthians see the apostles conversely as those of low status,[66] Paul also highlights with commendation the way in which Stephanas, the head of a household, sought to use himself and his assets in support of the church, rather than in furtherance of his own status, and, indeed, works on what appears to be terms of equality with those who may well have been his slaves.[67]

Euodia and Syntyche possibly had 'belonged to a team of men and women evangelizers'.[68] Cotter suggests that Paul's letter reflects both the respect and deference he has for these two women.[69] Furthermore, Apphia, mentioned in Philemon 2, may have been one of the leaders of the church at Colossae.[70] The list of names at the start of the letter does not necessitate the assumption that Apphia is the wife of Philemon. Apphia and Archippus are mentioned together; and Apphia receives from Paul the same designation as Phoebe of Cenchreae. Where Timothy is repeatedly recognised as Paul's brother, Phoebe and Apphia are affectionately and honourably described as his sisters.[71] Cotter also suggests that Chloe, mentioned in 1 Corinthians 1:11, may also have been a significant member of the Corinthian Christian community.[72] It may be, in contrast, however, that the situation in Chloe's

---

[66] See A.D. Clarke, *Secular and Christian Leadership in Corinth*.

[67] Cf. A.D. Clarke, ' "Refresh the Hearts of the Saints" ', 287–9; idem, *Secular and Christian Leadership*, 126; idem, *Serve the Community*, 227; and Winter, *After Paul Left Corinth*, 184–205.

[68] Cotter, 'Women's Authority Roles', 353.

[69] Ibid.

[70] Ibid. 351.

[71] Rom. 16:1; Philem. 2. For occurrences of the phrase 'Timothy, our brother' see 2 Cor. 1:1; Col. 1:1; 1 Thess. 3:2; Philem 1. See Cotter, 'Women's Authority Roles', 354.

[72] Ibid. 351–2, 368.

household more closely parallels that of the household of Narcissus and Aristobulus (Rom. 16:10–11), in which case, Chloe may not have been a leading woman in the Christian congregation, although within her household there may have been believers.

Conclusion

A theology of inclusiveness is clearly expressed by Paul in his correspondence with a number of churches (Gal. 3:28; 1 Cor. 12:13; Col. 3:11; cf. also Eph. 2:13–16). My analysis of the onomastic evidence of individuals associated with the Roman Christian congregations suggests that this theology of inclusiveness is also consistently demonstrated in his greetings. These appear to be presented in such a way as to transcend all ethnic, social and gender barriers.

A wider reading of the Pauline corpus suggests that this theological stance is not only reflected in Paul's attitudes underlying Romans 16, but also in comments he makes at a number of points in other letters. We may conclude that Paul's theological stance on inclusivity was not merely a philosophical standpoint, but is reflected in the way in which he treated his fellow believers – Jew and Gentile, slave and free, male and female.

Bibliography

Brändle, R., and E.W. Stegemann, 'The Formation of the First "Christian Congregations" in Rome', in K.P. Donfried and P. Richardson (eds.), *Judaism and Christianity in First-Century Rome* (Grand Rapids: Eerdmans, 1998)

Brooten, B., ' "Junia ... Outstanding among the Apostles" (Romans 16:7)', in L. and A. Swidler (eds.), *Women Priests: A Catholic Commentary on the Vatican Declaration* (New York: Paulist Press, 1977)

Chapple, A.L., 'Local Leadership in the Pauline Churches: Theological and Social Factors in its Development. A Study based on 1 Thessalonians, 1 Corinthians and Philippians'. PhD diss., University of Durham, 1984

Clarke, A.D., 'Another Corinthian Erastus Inscription', *TynBul* 40 (1989), 293–301

—, ' "Refresh the Hearts of the Saints": A Unique Pauline Context?', *TynBul* 47 (1996), 277–300

—, *Secular and Christian Leadership in Corinth: A Socio-historical and Exegetical Study of 1 Corinthians 1–6* (Leiden: E.J. Brill, 1993)

—, *Serve the Community of the Church: Christians as Leaders and Ministers* (Grand Rapids: Eerdmans, 2000)

Collins, J.N., *Diakonia: Re-interpreting the Ancient Sources* (Oxford: Oxford University Press, 1990)

Cotter, W., 'Women's Authority Roles in Paul's Churches: Countercultural or Conventional?', *NovT* 36 (1994), 350–72

Donfried, K.P., 'A Short Note on Romans 16', in K.P. Donfried (ed.), *The Romans Debate* (Edinburgh: T. & T. Clark, 1991)

Donfried, K.P., and P. Richardson (eds.), *Judaism and Christianity in First-Century Rome* (Grand Rapids: Eerdmans, 1998)

Fitzmyer, J.A., *Romans: A New Translation with Introduction and Commentary* (AB; New York: Doubleday, 1993)

Gamble, H., *The Textual History of the Letter to the Romans: A Study in Textual and Literary Criticism* (Grand Rapids: Eerdmans, 1977)

Guarducci, M., *Epigrafia greca IV. Epigrafi sacre pagane e christiane* (Rome: Instituto Poligrafico Dello Stato, 1978)

Holzapfel, R.C.N., 'Roman Christianity: The Congregations behind Romans 16'. PhD diss., Irvine, University of California, 1996

Horsley, G.H.R., *New Documents Illustrating Early Christianity* vol. 4 (North Ryde, NSW: Macquarie University, 1987)

Kearsley, R.A., 'Women in the World of the New Testament', *Ancient Society: Resources for Teachers* 15 (1985), 124–37; revised as 'Women in Public Life in the Roman East: Iunia Theodora, Claudia Metrodora and Phoebe, Benefactress of Paul', *TynBul* 50 (1999) 189–211

Lampe, P., *Die stadtrömischen Christen in den ersten beiden Jahrhunderten: Untersuchungen zur Sozialgeschichte* (Tübingen: J.C.B. Mohr, 1989)

—, *From Paul to Valentinus: Christians at Rome in the First Two Centuries* (Minneapolis: Fortress Press, forthcoming)

—, 'Iunia/Iunias: Sklavenherkunft im Kreise der corpaulinischen Apostel (Röm. 16:7)', *ZNW* 76 (1985), 132–4

—, 'The Roman Christians of Romans 16', in K.P. Donfried (ed.), *The Romans Debate* (Edinburgh: T. & T. Clark, 1991)

Oster, R.E., ' "Congregations of the Gentiles" (Rom 16:4): A Culture-based Ecclesiology in the Letters of Paul', *Restoration Quarterly* 40 (1998), 39–52

Pallas, D.I., S. Charitonidis and J. Venencie, 'Inscriptions lyciennes trouvées à Solômos près de Corinthe', *Bulletin de correspondance hellénique* 83 (1959), 496–508 = *SEG* 18 (1962), 143

Petersen, N.R., 'On the Ending(s) to Paul's Letter to Rome', in B.A. Pearson (ed.), *The Future of Early Christianity* (Minneapolis: Fortress Press, 1991)

Reasoner, M., *The Strong and the Weak: Romans 14:1–15:13 in Context* (SNTSMS 103; Cambridge: Cambridge University Press, 1999)

Romaniuk, K., 'Was Phoebe in Romans 16,1 a Deaconess?' *ZNW* 81 (1990), 132–4

Theissen, G., *The Social Setting of Pauline Christianity: Essays on Corinth* (Edinburgh: T. & T. Clark, 1982)

Thorley, J., 'Junia, a Woman Apostle', *NovT* 38 (1996), 18–29

Whelan, C.F., 'Amica Pauli: The Role of Phoebe in the Early Church', *JSNT* 49 (1993), 67–85

Winter, B.W., *After Paul Left Corinth: The Influence of Secular Ethics and Social Change* (Grand Rapids: Eerdmans, 2001)

5

God's Sovereignty over Roman Authorities: A Theme in Philippians[1]

Peter Oakes

Paul sits in a Roman prison, waiting for trial on a capital charge. He writes to his close friends at Philippi who are suffering at the hands of fellow townspeople and Roman colonial magistrates. It is little surprise that he writes the letter that he does: a letter whose body begins with an assertion that the gospel flourishes despite Roman imprisonment; a letter that ends by highlighting the establishment of a Christian group among the people at the very heart of the Roman empire. Paul's letter to the Philippians assures its hearers that God is sovereign over the Roman authorities under whom they are suffering. By doing this, Paul encourages them to stand firm for the gospel.

In my book *Philippians: From People to Letter* I argued that Paul presented himself as a model of the right attitude to have under suffering.[2] I think that we can be more specific about a major component of his attitude, namely confidence in God's sovereignty over his imprisonment. I also suggested that Christ was presented in such a way that he relativised the Roman emperor. I said that the point of this was to relativise the social imperatives that opposed the unity Paul wanted in the Philippian church.[3] However, it is clear that the presentation of Christ also strongly implies God's

---

[1] I would like to thank Sean Winter and Todd Klutz for their helpful comments on this chapter.

[2] Peter Oakes, *Philippians*, ch. 4.

[3] Ibid. chs. 5, 6.

sovereignty over the Roman authorities. If we take this sovereignty as a theme, it binds together the two types of passage: about Paul and about Christ. This theme is also highly relevant for the suffering Philippian church.

Paul's Situation and the Philippians' Situation

Paul

Paul is 'in chains' (1:7), either literally or in the broader sense of being under arrest. He is in constant contact with 'The Praetorium' (1:13). As J.B. Lightfoot argues, this expression usually refers to the Praetorian Guard at Rome.[4] Paul seems to be under military arrest.[5] He is also facing the possibility of execution. He writes of 'my eager expectation and hope that I will in no way be brought to shame but ... Christ will be glorified in my body, whether through life or through death' (1:20 cf. 1:21; 2:17; 3:10; my trans.).

Lightfoot's argument supports the traditional view, that Paul is at Rome, writing in the early sixties. This is reinforced by the existence of a significant number of Christians among 'Caesar's household' (4:22): the slaves, freedmen and freedwomen who formed the bulk of the imperial 'civil service'. There were far more of these at Rome than elsewhere. The counter-argument that Rome is too far from Philippi for the speed of journeys presupposed by the letter is not persuasive. We have little basis for estimating the time between the events that frame the necessary journeys: Epaphroditus's arrival at Paul's location (4:18) and his return to Philippi. However, even if Paul is at Ephesus or Caesarea, the important point is that his imprisonment is under the Roman authorities.

---

[4] J.B. Lightfoot, *St. Paul's Epistle to the Philippians,* 99–102. This conclusion, as opposed to the alternative view that the term refers to a building such as a governor's palace, is strengthened by the fact that the next words, 'and to all the others', refer to people rather than a place (Peter T. O'Brien, *Commentary on Philippians,* 93).

[5] Brian Rapske, *The Book of Acts and Paul in Roman Custody,* 28–32.

The Philippians

The Philippian Christians have been suffering for their faith. Paul writes that they will undoubtedly receive salvation (1:28) 'because it has been granted to you, on Christ's behalf, not only to believe in him but also to suffer for his sake' (1:29; my trans.). Paul then likens their suffering to his. He says that they are 'having the same struggle that you saw me face and now hear of me facing' (1:30 cf. 1:7; 2:17–18; 3:17–18; 4:9; my trans.). What they saw him face at Philippi was 'suffering and ill-treatment' (1 Thess. 2:2), almost certainly at the hands of the authorities (Acts 16:19–39). What they now hear of him facing is what has just been described in Philippians 1:12–26: Roman imprisonment on a capital charge.

We should not conclude that the Philippians were all in prison. This would be alien to Roman penal practice[6] and, in any case, opposition to Christians could not have taken such an organised form at such an early point. On the other hand, it is implausible that 'those who oppose' the Philippian Christians (and are in danger of 'panicking' them: 1:28) are, say, merely Jewish or Gentile false teachers. The Philippians' suffering is tangible, is in some way comparable to Paul's, and, as the rhetoric of the letter implies at several points, could lead to death (Paul uses himself and Christ as models of the right attitude for facing this: 1:20–3; 2:8; 2:17–18; 3:10–11). In a moderate-sized Roman colonial country town, halfway through the first century, the most likely form that 'suffering on behalf of Christ' would take is trouble, of various kinds, from non-Christian relatives, neighbours and other associates, exacerbated by occasional judicial punishment brought about when Christians become a focus of disturbances. I argued in *Philippians: From People to Letter* that the most prevalent long-term suffering would be economic. First-generation Christians had abandoned the gods of their family, trade and city to join a new, unknown Jewish sect. The perception of this as insulting, disloyal and shameful would lead to the breaking of many economically vital relationships, both within and beyond the family. This effect would be reinforced once some Christians were publicly perceived as troublemakers.[7] This all fits

---

[6] See ibid. 16–20, on the complexities of this issue.

[7] Oakes, *Philippians*, 89–96. The book also provides discussion of the views of scholars whose approaches differ from those of this chapter.

Paul's passionate plea for practical mutual support among the
Christians (2:1–4): 'each of you looking not to your own interests
but rather[8] to those of others' (2:4; my trans.). It also fits his reinforce-
ment of this plea with the example of Christ Jesus who underwent
the deepest possible loss of status and stayed obedient through
the worst possible suffering (2:6–8). For suffering first-generation
Christians, the economic rearrangement needed for mutual support
and survival was socially disturbing and dangerous.[9]

The Sovereignty of the Gospel over Paul's Imprisonment (1:12–26)

The beginning of the body of a letter is a key point for understanding its central concern. Paul turns immediately to asserting
the progress of the gospel in his imprisonment. As Loveday
Alexander argues, it is unsurprising that in a 'family letter' (or, as
Gordon Fee and others describe it, a 'letter of friendship'), such as
Philippians, the first main topic involves telling the recipients
about the sender's situation.[10] However, it is unusual for Paul to do
this, even in a letter to close friends (1 Thess.) or when he is in
prison (Philem.). Moreover, Paul does not tell the Philippians
much news about his situation itself. His interest is in the gospel.
In verses 12–26 Paul makes a series of points that demonstrate that
the gospel is sovereign over every aspect of his imprisonment.
The interests of the gospel determine everything that happens or
can happen. All those involved in Paul's situation are simply
subject to these interests.

Roman chains cannot bind the gospel (1:12–14)

The Philippian Christians are in danger of buckling under their
suffering and not standing firm for the gospel faith (cf. 1:27–9).

---

[8]   This translation of the word καί here is offered by Markus Bockmuehl
(*The Epistle to the Philippians*, 113–14).
[9]   Oakes, *Philippians*, 99–102, 188–201.
[10]   Loveday Alexander, 'Hellenistic Letter-Forms and the Structure of
Philippians', 92, 95; Gordon D. Fee, *Paul's Letter to the Philippians*, 2–4.

Paul's first response to this is to show that the gospel flourishes under pressure from the Roman authorities. He expects this to be a surprise to his hearers: note the μᾱλλον (rather) in verse 12. The ways in which it happens are also surprising. First, Paul sees the spread, among Roman authorities, of the knowledge that he is suffering for Christ as itself being great progress for the gospel (v. 13). Second, his imprisonment has made other Christians trust more in the Lord and tell the gospel more boldly (v. 14).

The first of these redefines the experience of any Philippians who have been punished by magistrates and have become publicly known as trouble-making Christians. Paul reverses Roman social expectations by giving such notoriety a positive, rather than negative, value.[11] The news of Christ's Lordship and salvation needs to be spread and their troubles inevitably spread it! Attempts by the Roman authorities to clamp down on the gospel will intrinsically have the opposite effect because they make it more widely known – and known in places, such as the Praetorium, that it might otherwise never penetrate. The second method of progress, of encouraging others to speak, is not so inevitable. Paul's declaration that the gospel is flourishing around him is probably intended to reveal to the Philippians that this is possible, and hence to encourage them to see the faithful suffering of their fellow Christians at Philippi (and of Paul at Rome) as being a ground for deepened trust in the Lord and therefore a motive for bolder evangelism, despite the authorities. The suffering engenders a kind of faithfulness that can enable boldness.

Attempts to prejudice Paul's trial promote the gospel (1:15–18a)

Further surprises follow. Paul now unpacks his statement about Christians in Rome speaking the word boldly, and the first comment he makes is that some of them are doing it out of envy and as a form of strife (v. 15). He admits that some preach out of good will and love (vv. 15–16,) but his focus is on those who 'proclaim Christ' from selfish ambition, 'thinking to stir up trouble for my chains' (v. 17). These Christians regard Paul negatively. Maybe they disagree with aspects of his views or practice. Or

---

[11] Rapske, *Custody,* 298.

perhaps they see his arrival in Rome as something of a threat. They engage in evangelism but do so in a way calculated (as Paul sees it) to cause him trouble. Presumably, the point at which such trouble would take effect would be at his forthcoming trial. The evangelism might prejudice the outcome. I suppose that something like the painting of Christian graffiti in prominent places would be the kind of activity that might have that consequence.[12] Paul sees their activity, interprets it as aggression towards him, and still rejoices because some sort of extra evangelistic work is going on (v. 18). Paul laughs, because even his Christian opponents' aim to cause trouble for his trial has become a cause of increased proclamation of the gospel.

Why put this in the letter? The most likely reason is that a related problem worries the Philippians. Since some Christians at Philippi are suffering, it would seem possible that the church there would be worried about trouble that continued evangelism might stir up for the sufferers. Paul's comments would then be particularly apposite: he rejoices in the spread of the gospel even if it is actually done deliberately to stir up trouble for him. On that basis, fear of the consequences for suffering church members should certainly not prevent the Philippians from seeking to proclaim the gospel.

Even Paul's execution would glorify Christ (1:18b–21)

Not only do Paul's imprisonment and the trouble-making tactics of his opponents cause the spread of the gospel, but he is confident that even in his death he would glorify Christ (v. 20). The bases he gives for this confidence are particularly relevant for the Philippians since they are not special to him as an apostle but are ones they already have, namely their own prayers and the help of the Holy Spirit (v. 19). These give Paul an 'eager expectation and hope' of the glorification of Christ through Paul's death. The apostle describes this outcome as his σωτηρία, 'salvation'. The echo of Job 13:16 in the phrase suggests that the word might have a connotation of 'vindication' here. A possible meaning of σωτηρία which could fit

---

[12] For the range of types of graffiti that could adorn a Roman town see J.-A. Shelton, *As the Romans Did*, 98–9.

here is 'preservation of character (as a Christian)'.[13] Probably a confidence of salvation in the sense of life after death would also flow from this (cf. 2:8–9; 3:10–11).

Even if the Roman authorities go to the limit of their judicial powers, the gospel is still there, waiting to be honoured as Christ is magnified. The Philippians need not fear suffering, because the sharpest form it could take would still glorify Christ and bring their salvation.

The gospel overrules the Roman judicial process (1:22–6)

In verses 22–6, Paul weighs up the question of whether his trial will result in execution or release. Astonishingly, neither the court, the judge, the witnesses, the evidence, nor the Roman authorities in any form, make any appearance. The sole arbiter of the outcome of Paul's trial is the gospel and its priorities.

This all comes as a surprise because, in verses 20–1, Paul seems to have been writing the more conventional things that one might expect a courageous and faith-filled potential martyr to write, 'I am confident that I will die in a way that glorifies Christ; life is for Christ and death is gain.' However, in verses 22–3, the apostle slides into an ambiguous rhetorical conversation in which he acts as though it is his choice how the trial ends. He weighs up the options and decides in favour of dying. But this is not the end of the matter. In verses 24–5 it becomes clear that his choice is not actually what decides the outcome. Rather, the deciding factor is what benefits the Philippians. Paul knows what this is, so he knows what the outcome of his trial will be!

The furthering of the gospel, in this case among the Philippians, determines the outcome of the Roman judicial process. The Roman authorities have no say in the matter. We can probably add to this an implication of verse 16. Paul writes, κεῖμαι – 'I am put here' or 'I am destined' – for the defence of the gospel. This refers either to his imprisonment as a whole or his trial in particular. In either case, an implication is that it is God who determined that the imprisonment should happen. God determines both the

---

[13] See the discussion of Epictetus, *Dissertationes* 4.1.163–7, in P. Oakes, 'Epictetus (and the New Testament)', 42–3.

imprisonment and the outcome. God is sovereign over the Roman authorities and all that they do to Paul.

The Philippians

In the letter to the Philippians, far more than in any other letter, Paul ties his hearers' experience to his and calls on them to imitate his attitudes and actions: 'in my chains and in the defence and confirmation of the gospel you are all sharers with me in grace' (1:7; my trans.); 'having the same struggle that you saw me face and now hear of me facing' (1:30); 'Be imitators of me … and look at those who live according to the pattern you have in us' (3:17); 'the things you learned and received and heard and saw in me – put these things into practice' (4:9). The things Paul presents in the letter, that the Philippians could imitate, are his attitude to his imprisonment and, in chapter 3, his willingness to lose privileges and face suffering. It is almost certain that Paul describes his views on his imprisonment to the suffering Philippians in order for them to adopt the views as their own. This conclusion is further strengthened by the way in which Paul also uses Christ as a model (2:5). In fact, not only does the apostle's Christological material reinforce his modelling of suffering; it also elevates the idea of God's sovereignty over the Roman authorities to a far higher level.

The Sovereignty of Christ over Roman Society (1:6, etc.; 2:9–11; 3:20–1)

We now move to passages in which no one would doubt that sovereignty is asserted. These are the description of Christ's accession to universal authority in 2:9–11 and the references to his final triumph, both in 3:20–1 and more broadly in the 'Day of Christ' texts such as 1:6. Paul draws the Philippians' attention to the sovereignty of Christ in a marked manner – and in ways reminiscent of the Roman emperor.

The Isaianic triumph of God, in Christ, over the Roman empire (and everywhere else) (2:9–11)

Either Paul has adopted 2:9–11 because he sees it as being relevant to the Philippians or, more probably, he has written it himself for the occasion.[14] The passage is a rewriting of the Septuagint of Isaiah 45:23: ἐμοὶ κάμψει ὅαν γόνυ καὶ ἐξομολογήσεται πᾶσα γλῶσσα τῷ θεῷ (to me every knee shall bow and every tongue shall confess to God). This rewriting of the Isaiah text is radical in several directions. The most startling is the replacing of God by Jesus as the figure bowed down to. The 'confession' then consists of acknowledgement that Jesus Christ is Lord. The Isaiah passage is among the most emphatically monotheistic in Scripture. In a vision intended for the exiles in Babylon, God sits on his throne and calls 'those from the end of the earth' to turn to him and be saved (Is. 45:22). He declares the uselessness of idols (45:20) and hence his uniqueness as saviour (45:21) and God: 'I am God, and there is no other' (45:22; my trans.). Paul sees this gathering and submission before God's throne as being fulfilled in Jesus. More particularly, it is fulfilled in Jesus' accession to universal sovereignty.

Paul clearly does not see this as a negation of the Isaianic vision. He makes God the chief actor in the scene (Phil. 2:9) and the ultimate recipient of glory through what happens (2:11).[15] Christ's accession to authority is the actualisation of God's sovereignty.[16] If we can pick up the earlier element in Isaiah 45, Christ's accession also actualises God's salvation. (If this element is there, then Paul would presumably have seen 'those from the end of the earth' as fulfilled in the Gentiles gathered in through the Christian mission.) Christ's accession to authority is the actualisation of God's sovereignty over the nations, such as Babylon, who imposed their authority on Israel.

However, the second aspect of the rewriting of Isaiah is that Jesus' sovereignty is not only over the nations but over the whole universe. This is part of a consistent pattern of extremes in

---

[14] Oakes, *Philippians*, 207–10.

[15] Contra D. Seeley, 'The Background of the Philippians Hymn (2.6–11)', 49–72; Internet edn, 3.

[16] R. Bauckham, 'The Worship of Jesus', 121.

Philippians 2:6–11. Christ moves from the highest status possible to the lowest (2:6–7). He suffers the worst death possible (2:8). He is given the highest name possible and the widest authority possible (2:9–10).

The third aspect of rewriting is the depiction of the accession of the figure to the Isaianic throne. The throne is not timelessly occupied but comes to be occupied. Along with this change comes a reference to the reason why this person comes to occupy the throne (note the 'therefore' in 2:9). This also functions as a legitimation of the authority of the one on the throne.

To some extent these changes could be seen simply as further implications of the core change of Jesus being on God's throne. This is especially so since the narrative needs to have a link to get from Jesus' death to his universal authority. However, neither description nor legitimation of the process of Jesus gaining authority is a normal feature of New Testament discourse. The explanation of these unusual features is probably to be found in the parallel process that happens in 3:20–1 (see below) where ideas about the parousia are rewritten in a form that deliberately evokes ideas about the Roman emperor.

Once the parallel process in 3:20–1 is seen, and the broader Roman references in Philippians are noted, then 2:9–11 too begins to look evocative of the Roman emperor. Jesus can be seen both to take on the central function of the emperor and to have his authority legitimated in a way familiar from Roman imperial ideology.

The function that Jesus takes on is the bringing of universal submission to a single head. This was consistently presented to the Roman provinces as the central benefit brought by the emperor. He alone could make the world function rationally and peacefully by bringing it under a single authority. For example, Philo writes of Augustus 'who reclaimed every state to liberty, who led disorder into order … He was also the first and the greatest and the common benefactor in that he displaced the rule of many and committed the ship of the commonwealth to be steered by a single pilot … "It is not well that many lords should rule." '[17]

---

[17] Philo, *De Legatione ad Gaium* 147–9. See Oakes, *Philippians*, 160–5; cf. E. Faust, *Pax Christi et Pax Caesaris*, esp. 475.

Jesus achieves everything that the emperor does in this but goes beyond him by doing it for the entire universe, including even the world of the dead.

The legitimation that supports Jesus' authority is the moral one of demonstrating both lack of self-interest and concern for others. He chose not to exploit his equality with God (2:6,)[18] a decision whose consequence was that he became like people (twice in 2:7). Moral legitimation of the emperor's rule was a central plank of the public presentation of imperial ideology. Concern for others and lack of self-interest were particularly prominent in such legitimation. Seneca writes, 'God says: "Let these men be kings because their forefathers have not been, because they have regarded justice and unselfishness as their highest authority, because, instead of sacrificing the state to themselves, they have sacrificed themselves to the state." '[19]

How might a depiction of Christ acceding to an authority beyond that of the Roman emperor help the Philippians? Essentially, it remaps the universe. Just as, later, 2:15–16 remaps Philippian society, moving the Christians from a despised, peripheral place to the core position of light and life, so 2:9–11 moves a crucified Jew to the centre of authority, relegating all competing authorities to places beneath him. In particular, the emperor, and hence the Philippian authorities and Philippian society as a whole, are relegated to a lower place. The immediate effects of this reinforce Paul's call to act for practical unity in the way shown by Christ's willingness to lose status and suffer obediently. The world has changed: it is now under Christ. Therefore Christ's imperatives of unity outweigh society's imperatives of cautious status preservation. Conversely, the security that Christ now offers outweighs that offered by society. As Paul implies in 2:12 the apparently suicidal path of unity and suffering is actually the way to bring about their individual and corporate salvation (cf. 3:10–11).[20]

---

[18] R.W. Hoover, 'The Harpagmos Enigma', 95–119; N.T. Wright, *The Climax of the Covenant*, 62–90.

[19] Seneca, *De Beneficiis* 4.32.2. See Oakes, *Philippians*, 154–60.

[20] Oakes, *Philippians*, 204–7.

Leaving these points aside, the key implication of 2:9–11 for this chapter is the simpler one that it places Christ above the Roman authorities. The enthronement of Christ brings about God's sovereignty over them. The Philippian Christians can with confidence stand firm because the one they follow is in authority over the colonial magistrates.

My reading of 2:9–11 has links with that of Dieter Georgi. The sharpest point of difference is that he sees the verses as comparable to an emperor's apotheosis after death, whereas I see them as comparable to an enthronement.[21] Christ is now in the position of reigning, rather than receiving reward for his past reign. Gordon Fee sees a contrast with 'lord Nero' in 2:9–11: the Christians have refused to participate in the imperial cult and God's exaltation of Christ vindicates their action.[22] I agree with many of Fee's general points about encouraging suffering Christians[23] and I agree that 2:9–11 does relativise the imperial cult. However, I see little evidence that the imperial cult itself is the key problem at Philippi. Richard Horsley argues that every presentation of the emperor is entangled with the imperial cult since that was the essential form of imperial ideology.[24] However, a writer can still make points about the emperor other than cultic ones. The emperor stands at the head of a social order and an authority structure. The overall content of Philippians suggests that these, rather than cultic issues *per se*, are more likely to be the target of 2:9–11 when interpreted as part of the letter.

To return to the question of authorship of 2:9–11, the familiarity of Isaiah 45:23 to Paul is seen from his use of it in Romans 14:11. Indeed, his straightforward interpretation of it there in terms of the judgement seat of God emphasises how unusual is his handling of it in Philippians. This could act as evidence of the non-Pauline origin of 2:9–11. However, the overall pattern of 'Roman' texts in Philippians, and the pertinence of 2:6–8 to the Philippians' circumstances, suggest to me that 2:9–11 is composed especially to help the Philippians in their situation.

---

[21] D. Georgi, *Theocracy in Paul's Praxis and Theology*, 73.

[22] Fee, *Philippians*, 31–2, 197.

[23] Ibid. 222–3.

[24] R. Horsley (ed.), *Paul and Empire*, 4, 17, 21, 22.

The triumphant return of the Lord Jesus Christ (3:20–1; 1:6, etc.)

In announcing the submission of every creature to Jesus, Philippians 2:9–11 is intrinsically political. If anything, 3:20–1 is still more sharply political because its explicit aim is to realign current allegiance. Also, the parallels between Christ and the Roman emperor are unmistakable. The Philippian Christians belong to a state elsewhere.[25] It is a place from which a 'saviour' who is the 'lord' will come to rescue them. This transforming rescue will happen 'in accordance with the power that enables him also to subject all things to himself' (my trans.). The Christians are like members of a colony such as Philippi, defended from a distance by the ruler of the city to which they ultimately belong. Moreover, their belonging to that city defines their ethics. Almost every element of this recalls Rome and the emperor.[26]

Citizenship (although not using that word) of heaven is contrasted with citizenship on earth, which leads to a mind focused on earthly things (3:20; cf. 3:19). This must have evoked the idea of the Roman citizenship that was held by many of the people of Philippi including, no doubt, a significant number of the Christians. Roman citizenship was supposed to define one's ethics.[27] Paul proclaims heavenly citizenship that implies different ethics. For Christian Roman citizens this relocates their place of primary allegiance. For probably most of the Philippian Christians, who are not Roman citizens,[28] Paul announces a citizenship that surpasses the citizenship of Rome and Philippi, which they are prevented from attaining. One effect of this is to put all the Christians in Philippi on a level with each other. This could itself help Paul's call for unity in the church.

Philippians 3:20–1 holds a structurally important place in the letter. The chapter break after it is misleading. Paul's announcement of Christ's use of his universal authority to return to rescue his people forms the final climax of his main message to the Philippians. He concludes, with a great rhetorical flourish: 'Thus,

---

[25] Cf. ibid. 140.

[26] Oakes, *Philippians*, 138–45.

[27] Cicero, *de Legibus* 2.2.5.

[28] Oakes, *Philippians*, 62–3.

my beloved and longed-for brothers and sisters, my joy and my crown, in this way stand firm in the Lord, my beloved ones' (4:1; my trans.). The promise of Christ's triumphant return caps the argument. In fact, at the ends of previous sections too Paul has tended to lead the argument to that return, with references to 'the Day of Christ' (1:10; 2:16). A key element of the apostle's call for the Philippians to stand firm is his teaching of Christ's final sovereignty, a sovereignty that will be used to rescue his people. Again, this fulfils a central function of the Roman emperor. If the emperor's key function towards the *provinces* was the bringing of universal submission to a single head, his key function towards the *Roman people* was to be the one who would save them from their enemies and from internal trouble.[29]

The Christians have a better citizenship than that of Rome, defended by a stronger saviour than that of Rome. On this basis, the Philippian church can confidently stand firm under their sufferings, assured of Christ's final sovereignty.

Conclusions

Paul remaps the universe and consequently remaps both Philippian society and the future. Rome, the emperor (and even Jupiter) are replaced in the positions of decisive authority by Christ. Paul urges the Philippians to look at their world and see a new reality: to look even at imprisonment and other suffering and see, even in those settings, the reality of God's sovereignty. Paul urges them to look at the future and see it as the implementation and final fulfilment of Christ's sovereignty. This rounded presentation of God's sovereignty over the authorities everywhere, from the apostle's prison to the courts of the universe, gives a firm basis for Philippian courage and steadfastness on behalf of the Christian gospel.

---

[29] J. Béranger, *Recherches sur l'aspect idéologique du Principat*, 254–78; Oakes, *Philippians*, 138–45.

Bibliography

Alexander, Loveday, 'Hellenistic Letter-Forms and the Structure of Philippians', *JSNT* 37 (1989), 87–101

Bauckham, R., 'The Worship of Jesus', in Ralph P. Martin and Brian J. Dodd (eds.), *Where Christology Began: Essays on Philippians 2* (Louisville, KY: Westminster / John Knox Press, 1998)

Béranger, Jean, *Recherches sur l'aspect idéologique du Principat* (Basel: Reinhardt, 1953)

Bockmuehl, Markus, *The Epistle to the Philippians* (London: A. & C. Black, 1997)

Faust, E., *Pax Christi et Pax Caesaris: Religionsgeschichtliche, traditionsgeschichtliche u. Sozialgeschichtliche Studien zum Epheserbrief* (Freiburg: Universitätsverlag / Göttingen: Vandenhoeck & Ruprecht, 1993)

Fee, Gordon D., *Paul's Letter to the Philippians* (NICNT; Grand Rapids: Eerdmans, 1995)

Georgi, Dieter, *Theocracy in Paul's Praxis and Theology*, trans. D.E. Green (Minneapolis: Fortress Press, 1991 [Ger. 1987])

Hoover, R.W., 'The Harpagmos Enigma: A Philological Solution', *HTR* 64 (1971), 95–119

Horsley, R. (ed.), *Paul and Empire: Religion and Power in Roman Imperial Society* (Harrisburg: Trinity Press International, 1997)

Lightfoot, J.B., *St. Paul's Epistle to the Philippians* (London: Macmillan, 1885)

O'Brien, Peter T., *Commentary on Philippians* (NIGTC; Grand Rapids: Eerdmans, 1991)

Oakes, Peter, 'Epictetus (and the New Testament)', *Vox Evangelica* 23 (1993), 39–56

—, *Philippians: From People to Letter* (SNTSMS 110; Cambridge: Cambridge University Press, 2001)

Philo, *De Legatione ad Gaium* 147–9, *On the Embassy to Gaius*, trans. F.H. Colson (Loeb; London: Heinemann, 1962)

Rapske, Brian, *The Book of Acts and Paul in Roman Custody* (A1CS 3; Carlisle: Paternoster Press / Grand Rapids: Eerdmans, 1994)

Seeley, David, 'The Background of the Philippians Hymn (2.6–11)', *Journal of Higher Criticism* 1 (fall 1994), 49–72; Internet edn at http://daniel.drew.edu/~doughty/jhcbody.html#reviews

Seneca, *De Beneficiis, Moral Essays*, vol. 3, trans. J.W. Basore (Loeb; Cambridge, MA: Harvard University Press, 1935)

Shelton, J.-A., *As the Romans Did: A Sourcebook in Roman Social History* (Oxford: Oxford University Press, 1998²)

Wright, N.T., *The Climax of the Covenant: Christ and the Law in Pauline Theology* (Edinburgh: T. & T. Clark, 1991)

6

Disturbing Trajectories: *1 Clement*, the *Shepherd of Hermas* and the Development of Early Roman Christianity

Andrew Gregory

Introduction

Three recent studies[1] have attempted to trace the development of early Christianity at Rome on the basis of chronological trajectories they have drawn between Christian texts thought to shed light on the Christian community in that city.[2] The texts that mark the beginning and end of each trajectory are Paul's letter to the Romans, dated c. AD 58, and the letter from the Roman Christians to the Corinthians known as *1 Clement* and dated usually to c. AD 96.

The letter *1 Clement* is one of only two early Christian writings that may be said with certainty to originate at Rome; the other is the *Shepherd of Hermas*. The *Shepherd* is usually dated in the second century, and therefore receives less attention than *1 Clement* in

---

[1] R.E. Brown, *Antioch and Rome*, 87–216; W.L. Lane, 'Social Perspectives on Roman Christianity during the Formative Years from Nero to Nerva', 196–244; C.C. Caragounis, 'From Obscurity to Prominence', 245–79.

[2] J.M. Robinson introduced the term 'trajectory' into the study of early Christianity, using it to refer to the various lines of development that he detected there. Following Walter Bauer, he argued that there was no consistent straight-line development of early Christianity, and that orthodoxy was something imposed upon others by Christians at Rome. See J.M. Robinson and H. Koester (eds.), *Trajectories Through Early Christianity*, esp. 8–19.

studies of early Roman Christianity. My contention in this chapter is that the chronological framework that privileges *1 Clement* to the detriment of the *Shepherd of Hermas* is misconceived, for the conventional dates given to these texts rest more on scholarly reiteration than on historical evidence. So too I shall argue that both texts are of central importance in any attempt to catch glimpses of early Christianity at Rome as it may be reflected in Christian documentary sources. New Testament scholarship may tend to give more attention to canonical texts that may be from Rome, but the undisputed origin of *1 Clement* and the *Shepherd* in Rome means that they are of the utmost importance for the historical study of early Christianity at Rome.[3]

Therefore I shall seek to disturb recently proposed trajectories of the development of early Christianity at Rome in three ways. First, I shall argue that there is no good reason to date *1 Clement* to c. 96. Therefore it is not possible to assume that it was written one generation after Paul's letter to Rome. Any proposed trajectories that depend on this dating are therefore to be treated with scepticism. Second, I shall argue that to omit any discussion of the *Shepherd of Hermas* from discussions of early Christianity at Rome, even if those discussions are framed only by reference to the first century, is likely to result in a distorted and selective trajectory/reconstruction. The *Shepherd* may antedate or be contemporary with *1 Clement*, but even if it is later it affects any conclusions that might be drawn from *1 Clement* because the evidence of the *Shepherd* makes it difficult to see *1 Clement* as the end of a historical trajectory. Third, I shall argue that although their undisputed Roman origin means that *1 Clement* and the *Shepherd* should both be considered as of paramount importance as witnesses for the development of Christianity at Rome, nevertheless the nature of their testimony is such as to suggest that they shed very little light on concerns and issues that were specific to the city of Rome. Although their origin in Rome is undisputed, it is ironic that modern scholars would have no reason to locate these texts in Rome were it not for the way in which clearly, unambiguously and explicitly these texts locate themselves in

---

[3] Other canonical texts sometimes located in Rome include Philippians, Ephesians, Hebrews, James, 1 Peter and Mark. See Brown, 'Rome', 185–201, B.H. Streeter, *The Primitive Church*, 189–200.

that city.[4] They do shed light on 'Roman Christianity', in that they are shaped by the Roman cultural world in which they were written, but they do so primarily in a way that might be appropriate for any urban setting from Rome to the eastern boundaries of the empire rather than in a way that is necessarily distinctive to and characteristic of the city of Rome itself.[5]

Disturbing Trajectories: Dating *1 Clement* and the *Shepherd of Hermas*

Dating 1 Clement

Quite apart from any evidence that the text of *1 Clement* might be thought to provide for a reconstruction of early Christianity in Rome, the main reason for the centrality of this text in contemporary discussion is the belief that it may be dated with certainty to c. 96. This puts the letter about forty years after the writing of Paul's letter to the Romans, and the period of time that has elapsed between the two offers scholars a convenient space in which to plot a trajectory of development. Yet the arguments on which this dating rests are precarious, as has been demonstrated by L.L. Welborn[6] and T.J. Herron.[7] Lane[8] acknowledges that Welborn has reopened the question of the date of the composition of *1 Clement*, but his own restatement of the case for the commonly accepted dating fails to interact with Welborn's arguments, and he appears to make no reference to Herron. It is necessary therefore to give them the hearing that they deserve.

---

[4] The writer of *1 Clement* greets the church in Corinth in the name of the church in Rome in the letter's salutation. Hermas says that he was sold to Rhoda in Rome (Vis. 1.1) and refers to journeys to Cumae (Vis. 1.3, 2.1) and on the Via Campana (Vis. 4.1).

[5] On the ambiguity of the word 'Rome' to mean both city and empire, see M. Griffin, 'Urbs Roma, Plebs and Princeps', 19–22.

[6] L.L. Welborn, 'Date', 34–54.

[7] T.J. Herron, 'The Most Probable Date of the First Epistle of Clement to the Corinthians', 106–21.

[8] Lane, 'Formative Years', 226. Cf. Caragounis, 'Development', 265, n. 79.

Welborn's discussion of the date of Clement accepts the normal reading of most of the internal evidence of the text, and concludes from this that the letter is to be dated sometime after AD 80. Four indications of date support this *terminus a quo*: (1) The account of the death of Peter and Paul is not that of an eyewitness; (2) the presbyters whom the apostles installed have died (44.2) and 'a second ecclesiastical generation has also passed' (44.3); (3) the church at Corinth is called 'ancient' (47.6); and (4) the emissaries from Rome are said to have lived blamelessly as Christians 'from youth to old age' (63.3). 'Such statements', Welborn concludes 'relegate the epistle to the last decades of the first century',[9] that is, the 80s or 90s. The history of reception of the letter indicates its *terminus ad quem*; Hegesippus[10] appears to have seen the letter c. 150, and Dionysius of Corinth[11] refers to it shortly afterwards.

Yet there may be room to argue that the *terminus a quo* may be brought even further forward. Peter and Paul are described as examples not of old time (ἀρχαίων ὑποϖειγμάτων) but of the days nearest to us (ἔγγιστα) and of our own generation (5.1). Too much should not be inferred from these descriptions, as their primary purpose is to differentiate the present generation from the period of the Jewish Scriptures on which the author of the letter has drawn already. Yet nor should we ignore the proximity to the martyrdoms of Peter, Paul and others claimed by the writer. As Thomas Herron has argued,[12] the use of the superlative (ἔγγιστα) rather than the comparative does seem to suggest that the author intended to locate the martyrdoms of Peter and Paul as very close to his own time rather than merely closer to his time than his earlier named examples. It is true that nowhere does he claim to be an immediate contemporary of Peter and Paul, but nor is there good reason to believe that many years have passed since their deaths. They are part of the immediate history of the Christian community at Rome, and there is no reason to exclude a date from as early as even the late 60s or early 70s. This allows a sufficient lapse of time for the Neronian persecution to have

---

[9] Welborn, 'Date', 37.
[10] Eusebius, *Historia ecclesiastica* 3.16, 4.22.1.
[11] Ibid. 4.23.11.
[12] Herron, 'Most Probable Date', 114.

ended and for the church in Rome to be aware of that period as distinct from the current struggle engaging Christians at both Corinth and Rome.

The second argument for dating the letter is based on its reference to some of those whom the apostles appointed to office in Corinth having died and having been succeeded by others, and to the related statement that such individuals had served blamelessly for many years (44.2–3). Welborn infers from this that 'a second ecclesiastical generation has also passed',[13] but it is not quite clear how long a period the letter envisages. 'Many' might be interpreted in more than one way, for the word is vague and its meaning is dependent to some extent on its context. Herron argues that even ten or fifteen years might seem many to a church founded a mere twenty-five years before.[14] So too he notes that there is no reason to preclude a second generation of presbyters having been appointed in the 60s if some of their predecesors were already elderly at the time of their appointment in the 50s, and that this would allow the appointment of the second generation to have taken place in the 60s. This seems reasonable, so once again the *terminus a quo* is brought forward to c. 70.

The third argument rests on the letter's apparent reference to the age of the church at Corinth. This church, we are told, is ἀρχαίαν (47.6), but it is by no means certain how old this requires it to be. Presumably there is no reason to believe that its earliest members were ἀρχαίοι as were the ἀρχαίων ὑποδειγμάτων to whom the author refers in 4.1–13 (see 5.1), and it seems easier simply to assume that the church at Corinth was ἀρχαίαν because it goes back to the founding of the church at the beginning ἀρχή (47.2) of Paul's preaching. Ἀρχαίαν, like 'many', is a relative term, and it seems no more likely that a church of some fifty years' standing (assuming that the church in Corinth as founded in the mid-40s, and that the letter is dated c. 96) may be considered more ancient than a church of some twenty-five years' standing (assuming that the letter is dated c. 70). Herron provides further support for this reading of the text of *1 Clement* when he notes that Paul also uses the same phrase, ἐν ἀρχῇ τοῦ εὐαγγελίου (Phil. 4:15), to refer to

---

[13] Welborn, 'Date', 37.
[14] Herron, 'Most Probable Date', 113.

the period in which he preached to the Philippians after an interval of only ten years.[15]

The fourth argument rests not on inferences about the age of Christians at Corinth but on inferences about the age of Christians at Rome, for the Roman bearers of the letter are said to have lived faithfully 'among us' without blame from youth to old age (63.3). Welborn refers to this evidence as follows: 'the emissaries from Rome are said to have lived "blamelessly" as Christians "from youth to old age"'.[16] The form of Welborn's statement is significant, for he infers that the emissaries were Christians from their youth, as opposed to individuals who were long known to be of high character to the Christians in whose name the author writes, irrespective of when the emissaries began to follow Christ. This inference is unnecessary, so once again therefore Welborn's *terminus a quo* may be brought forward.

Thus far I have argued that a number of general statements in the letter tend to support a *terminus a quo* of c. 70,[17] and that the evidence of its reception supports a *terminus ad quem* of c. 140. However, the most important internal evidence relating to the traditional and precise date of c. 96 rests on a statement in the letter that is said to indicate that it was written just after a period of persecution had finished. This persecution is said to have occurred under Domitian who was emperor 81–96, so the letter is dated to just after his death. There are two problems with this dating. First, it is not clear that there was any particular persecution of Christians in Rome under Domitian.[18] Second, it is not clear that the letter makes reference to any persecution

---

[15] Ibid. 115.

[16] Welborn, 'Date', 37.

[17] Although Herron argues that c. 70 should be considered the most probable date, not the *terminus a quo*. His strongest argument for this is based on his understanding of the rhetoric of the letter: the author's argument for order on the basis of the Jerusalem temple only makes sense if the temple is still standing. Thus Herron suggests that references to the Jerusalem temple in the present tense in this letter are of a different nature from those in Josephus ('Most Probable Date', 108–10).

[18] For discussion and bibliography, see Welborn, 'Date', 40–4; D.E. Aune, *Revelation 1–5*, lxiv–lxix.

other than that associated with the deaths of Peter, Paul and a great multitude of the chosen (4.1 – 5.6).

The case that *1 Clement* refers to a period of persecution that has recently ended depends on a particular reading of the letter's opening remarks: Διὰ τὰς αἰφνίδιους καὶ ἐπαλλήλους γενομένας ἡμῖν συμφορὰς καὶ περιπτώσεις, βράδιον νομίζομεν ... (1.1). Kirsopp Lake's translation of this opening is as follows: 'Owing to the sudden and repeated misfortunes and calamities which have befallen us, we consider that our attention has been somewhat delayed in turning to the questions disputed among you ... (1.1)'.[19]

Three words in particular require comment. The first two are each present in the text: συμφορὰς, which Lake translates as 'misfortunes', and περιπτώσεις which he translates as 'calamaties'. Welborn draws attention to a tradition of scholarship that has commented on the vagueness of this language and that has questioned whether it may be taken to refer to persecution.[20] So too he offers a number of examples of the use of these words which demonstrate that they should be translated as 'events' or 'circumstances' and 'experiences' or 'accidents'. Thus he concludes that there is no linguistic evidence for interpreting these words as allusions to persecution, and that it is only under the influence of their belief in a persecution under Domitian that Lake and others have coloured this 'pallid hendiadys' in this way.[21] The third word to be considered is διωγμός, the usual word for 'persecution'. The letter does use this word when it refers to the Neronian persecution (3.2), but does not use it here. Were there firm independent evidence to suggest that there was persecution under Domitian and that *1 Clement* should be dated to his principate, then it might be possible to suggest that the present argument is an argument from silence. Yet this would be to misrepresent the point: what is important is not only that the letter fails to refer to persecution, but also that he makes use of a rhetorical *captatio benevolentiae*, which may be explained without reference to any alleged persecution.[22]

---

[19] K. Lake, *Apostolic Fathers*, vol. 1.
[20] Welborn, 'Date', 38–44.
[21] Ibid. 39.
[22] Ibid. 47.

This being so, there is no other reason to date the letter to the end of Domitian's life. Therefore there is no specific evidence on which to date *1 Clement,* and we can be no more confident than to conclude that it was probably written at some point in the period 70–140.

The Shepherd of Hermas in recent trajectories

The *Shepherd of Hermas* has not been altogether ignored in recent discussions of Christianity at Rome, and the three proposed trajectories to which I have referred each make mention of the book. Brown, who dates the work to the first half of the second century,[23] notes that its evidence may be fitted neatly into the trajectory of Roman Christianity that he has outlined, for this text brings the trajectory onwards into the second century.[24] Caragounis also dates the *Shepherd of Hermas* in the second century,[25] but although he suggests that it may be used – with care – to augment the evidence of *1 Clement* for the state of Christianity at Rome towards the end of the first century,[26] he seems to rule out this possibility by virtue of his concluding remarks about the letter. '*1 Clement*', he claims, 'shows that the time of creative Christian writing is over. The letter has nothing new to offer.'[27] This is a bold statement, for not only does it pass judgement on *1 Clement* but so too it requires the conclusion that other (later) texts will show no creativity.

Yet this seems to be untrue of the *Shepherd of Hermas.* Not only does it appear to take a different approach to the theology of post-baptismal sin from that evinced in Hebrews,[28] which suggests that the text exhibits theological creativity either independently of or in dialogue with Hebrews, but so too it appears to support

---

[23] Brown, 'Rome', 203–4.

[24] Ibid. 90.

[25] Caragounis, 'Development', 245, refers to the *Shepherd* as one of several texts that is later than the last forty years of the first century. At 266 he accepts the date 140–55.

[26] Ibid. 245.

[27] Ibid. 278.

[28] *Shepherd of Hermas*, Mand. 4.3, 31.1. Cf. Hebrews 6:4–6.

a model of ministry that includes the charismatic alongside the institutional.[29] Thus if the *Shepherd* is contemporary with or later than *1 Clement*, then it may call into question Caragounis's suggestion that *1 Clement* represents the repudiation of a charismatic or Pauline type of church government in favour of a more static model.[30] Caragounis maintains that *1 Clement* represents the whole of the Roman church, but the evidence of the *Shepherd* calls into question a trajectory that ends with a repudiation of charismatic ministry.

Dating the Shepherd of Hermas

Carolyn Osiek notes three pegs upon which hang all theories as to the date of the *Shepherd*.[31] All rely on evidence external to the text of the *Shepherd*. One is the claim, first made by Origen,[32] that the Hermas of Romans 16:14 is the author of the book. The second is the claim that the Clement to whom reference is made in Vision 2.4.3 may be identified with a Clement who can be dated from other evidence. The third is a reference to the *Shepherd* in the *Muratorian Fragment*.

The identification of the Clement identified as a scribe in Vision 2.4.3 with a known individual who may be dated independently should be rejected. Such theories, whether they argue that this Clement was the bishop listed by Irenaeus[33] or that he was associated with the household of Titus Flavius Clemens,

---

[29] Also relevant to the creativity of Hermas as a Christian theologian at Rome is his use of analogies that appear to reflect his Roman context rather than any biblical counterpart, such as the willow, the elm and the vine, and possibly the garment and the empty jars. See G.F. Snyder, *The Apostolic Fathers*, vol. 6: *The Shepherd of Hermas*, 17–18.

[30] Similarly Lane, 'Formative Years', 241, suggests that the Shepherd supports a marked development away from an earlier period in which leadership was a function of charismatic endowment. Lane's position is more nuanced than that of Caragounis, for his choice of words allows for both institutional and charismatic ministries to coexist, and this is what we find in the *Shepherd*.

[31] C. Osiek, *Shepherd of Hermas*, 18.

[32] Origen, *Commentarii in Romanos* 10.31.

[33] Irenaeus, *Adversus Haereses* 3.3.3. E.g. Brown, 'Rome', 162–4.

known to us from Suetonius,[34] associate the Clement of *1 Clement* with the Clement of the *Shepherd* because each is linked to a letter from Rome. Yet nowhere does the text of *1 Clement* mention Clement by name, and this title may be based on no more than an inference on the part of early Christians who read an anonymous letter from Rome as if it had been written by the Clement of the *Shepherd*.

Origen's statement that the Hermas of Romans 16:14 is the author of the *Shepherd* may also be the result of inference and wishful thinking. Thus Osiek notes that Origen may have made this claim because he wished to defend the book as inspired and therefore needed to situate it as early as possible.[35]

No less problematic is the third peg, the evidence of the *Muratorian Fragment*, although it seems clear that it is this evidence that has led the majority of scholars to date Hermas to the second century. This fragmentary and not unproblematic Latin text states that Hermas wrote the *Shepherd* very recently (*nuperrime*) while his brother Pius was bishop in Rome. Pius is known to us from Irenaeus,[36] and his episcopate is usually dated c. 140–54. There is some dispute about the date of the *Muratorian Fragment*. If a fourth-century date is accepted,[37] then its reference to the *Shepherd* is a fiction intended to make the fragment seem earlier than it is. Even if a second-century date is accepted,[38] its testimony is not altogether beyond dispute, however. Snyder notes that it is strange that the brother of a monarchical bishop seems to know only of a presbyterial organisation of the congregation, that there is no obvious persecution to which the book might refer, and that the *Muratorian Fragment* may have been influenced by Hippolytus, who wished to discredit the *Shepherd*.[39] None of these objections is

---

[34] Suetonius, *Domitian* 15. E.g. J.S. Jeffers, *Conflict at Rome*; Caragounis, 'Development', 266.

[35] Osiek, *Shepherd*, 18.

[36] Irenaeus, *Adversus Haereses* 3.3.3.

[37] So G.M. Hahneman, *The Muratorian Fragment and the Development of the Canon*.

[38] So E. Ferguson, review of Hahneman, 691–7. Cf. idem, 'Canon Muratori', 677–83.

[39] Snyder, *Shepherd*, 22–3.

compelling, however, even on a second-century date for the fragment. It is impossible to be certain when and how the transition to
a monarchical bishop came about at Rome, and Irenaeus may be
anachronistic in his listing of the episcopal succession in Rome; the
references to persecution seem vague, and might still point to the
remembrance of the Neronian persecution even after almost a
century; and doubts have been expressed as to whether the supposed influence of Hippolytus on the fragment rests on firm evidence.[40]

Various other internal arguments have been brought forward
to date the *Shepherd*.[41] None is compelling, but each tends to
favour an earlier date than that demanded by the evidence of the
Muratorian Fragment, if it is accepted. Theories of multiple authorship are able to take into account all three 'historical' references
discussed above,[42] although most scholars now favour single
authorship, perhaps in stages.[43] Osiek concludes cautiously that
the work should be dated to 'an expanded duration of time
beginning perhaps from the very last years of the first century, but
stretching through most of the first half of the second century',[44]
although in fact she offers no explanation as to why the *Shepherd*
may not be dated earlier in the first century.

There seems no reason why the *terminus a quo* need be any later
than some time after the Neronian persecution. Although Osiek
notes that Wilson's assumptions *about* the emergence of the
monarchical episcopate vitiates his argument for this early date,[45]
this affects only his *terminus ad quem*, for he believes that Hermas
must antedate the emergence of mono-episcopacy at Rome, and
he argues that this emerged with the accession of Clement to the

---

[40] J.C. Wilson, *Towards a Reassessment of the Shepherd of Hermas*, 29;
Hahneman, *Muratorian Fragment*, 55–6.

[41] See Wilson, *Reassessment*; H.O. Maier, *The Social Setting of the Ministry
as Reflected in the Writings of Hermas, Clement and Ignatius.*

[42] Osiek, *Shepherd*, 8–9.

[43] Ibid. 10.

[44] Ibid. 20.

[45] Wilson suggests late first century, possibly as early as 80 (*Reassessment*,
7), but offers the Neronian persecution as his *terminus a quo* (*Reassessment*,
59), which allows us to suggest that 70 is possible.

episcopacy c. 92–100. Therefore it seems most satisfactory to argue that the *Shepherd* should be dated to the period c. 70 to c. 150, and to note that if the evidence of the *Muratorian Canon* is discounted, then there are good reasons to favour the early part of this range.

Conflicting Trajectories: *1 Clement* and the *Shepherd of Hermas* as contemporary reflections of Christianity at Rome?

I have argued that both *1 Clement* and the *Shepherd* may each be dated no more precisely than to some point in the period 70–140. If this is accepted, then it means not only that they may each provide reflections of at least some contemporary expressions of Christianity at Rome, but also that each might antedate the other. If one antedates the other, then it may be possible to argue that any differences between them might be interpreted as evidence of the development of Christian ideas or practice over time in Rome. Thus *1 Clement* has been used to suggest that charismatic leadership has given way to institutional structures, although the *Shepherd* seems to give the lie to this as it depicts the charismatic prophet coexisting alongside the elders. Only if it is the earlier text is it possible to use it as evidence for a trajectory moving from prophetic to institutional structures.

If they are more or less contemporary, then any differences between them might be interpreted as evidence of diversity of practice or belief among Christians in Rome, whether those differences appear to be socio-economic, ethnic or in terms that might be loosely considered as theological. They may, for example, reflect the outlook of two different house churches regardless of what relationship, if any, there is between them. Whether they are contemporary or not, it seems clear that one cannot be used as the only window on to Christianity in Rome in the period 70–140, for the picture seen through one window will inevitably affect the picture seen through the other, even if it is only taken to demonstrate that the other picture is incomplete. The evidence of other texts that might come from Rome in the same period may be drawn on, albeit with caution, but *1 Clement* and the *Shepherd* each require prominent attention because they are the only texts whose origin at Rome is clear, even if their precise relationship to each other is not.

One corollary of this argument is that although the historical relationship between the two texts and their authors cannot be determined with any degree of confidence, nevertheless it may be possible to say something of the social setting of each text and to relate it to the social setting of the other. This is to ground each text in an urban world such as that of Rome, but leaves open questions of absolute and relative dating. Various studies have set out to do this, and there is much that can be said of the Roman cultural milieu in which they were written. For just as there are elements in the text that might be categorised for heuristic purposes as reflecting Jewish, Christian and Hellenistic influences,[46] so too there are elements that may be said to be distinctively Roman. We turn therefore to a discussion of what might be said about the Roman social world that may be reflected in these texts, before proceeding to question the extent to which that social world reflects and is indicative of Rome as a city rather than as the culture of an empire.

Remapping Trajectories: *1 Clement* as in and from but not (just) about Rome

The letter *1 Clement* is full of imagery that might be called Roman, whether in the emphasis on peace, concord,[47] order and stability in church, state and cosmos (20.1 – 21.1; 60.4, 61.1), in the metaphor of the army for an ordered church (37–8), or the submission of slave to master as a symbol of the peace and concord that comes when Christians submit to God. The writer also makes use of the phoenix as a picture of the resurrection (25).

---

[46] Although these influences were so thoroughly intermingled that they cannot be reseparated; the cultural mix of Rome and the particular influence of eastern ideas was proverbial at the end of the first century, e.g. Juvenal, *Satires* 3.

[47] On the Roman context of which see further Welborn, 'Date', 44–8; K. Wengst, *Pax Romana and the Peace of Jesus Christ*, 105–18.

Although such characteristics might be Roman, they are Roman in the sense of the culture of an empire, not distinct to any one city.[48] So too *1 Clement's* concern with the good management of the household (1.3) and his emphasis on hospitality as a virtue (1.2; 10.7; 11.1; 12.1) fit well with a situation in which the house church was the primary setting of the Christian community, although this is a setting that is likely to have been true throughout the empire. Equally, his familiarity with Jewish Scripture is consistent with the writer's location in Rome,[49] but might equally be true of Christian communities in other cities that had significant Jewish populations.

The writer appears also to be familiar with Romans, 1 Corinthians, Hebrews, and possibly James. Christological concerns are prominent, and the death of Jesus is important for his thought, though he shows no evidence of the use of Mark, sometimes associated (via Peter) with Rome, or indeed of any of the Gospels. Again, although these traits may be said to characterise a letter we can place at Rome, it is difficult to see how they are distinctive to or limited to that city.[50]

---

[48] Even in Galilee, we should remember, a Roman centurion could use the command structure of the Roman army as a parallel for the authority of Jesus (Luke 7), and a Hellenistic Jew (identified in Acts as a Roman citizen) called Paul could use Roman military imagery in a letter to a Roman city in the East (Eph. 6).

[49] D.A. Hagner, *The Use of the Old and New Testaments in Clement of Rome*, 21, notes that one quarter of his text is composed of scriptural citations.

[50] A possible exception might be that *1 Clement's* knowledge of Hebrews is distinctive at this early period. This could be supported by arguing that the *Shepherd*, Mand. 4.3.1–2, also shows knowledge of Hebrews, if his defence of post-baptismal repentance is taken as a direct rejection of the rigorist position of Hebrews 6:4–6. Justin Martyr, who taught at Rome, also seems to have known the letter. Yet it is hard to argue that a lack of evidence for the knowledge of the letter elsewhere prior to Irenaeus and Clement of Alexandria is significant. Similarly, a lack of evidence for the knowledge of Mark in early Christian writings is not in itself evidence against Mark being associated with Rome, just as the fact that Justin may have known this work is not in itself a significant connection between Mark and Rome; Justin is the first author in whose writings extensive Jesus traditions are to be found, and he had travelled widely in the East before settling in Rome.

On this evidence therefore it seems difficult to know what
1 Clement tells us of Christianity at Rome that is distinctive to that
city. Therefore it may be that to seek to move beyond a general
picture of a Christian community with strong Jewish influences in a
culturally Roman social milieu is to distort the evidence that we
have, and to limit and constrain what we can learn from *1 Clement*
as a text that points to continuity and communication between
Christian churches that exist within a culture common to Roman
cities across the Roman world. Therefore *1 Clement* is a text that
may shed light on continuity among early Christian communities
that may have been overlooked due to recent emphasis on the
diversity of early Christianity. That there was diversity seems
beyond doubt, but the author of *1 Clement* claims to be able to
appeal to shared belief in his appeal to the Corinthians.

Thus, although the text tells us little that may be said to be
distinctive of Christianity at Rome, it shows us a great deal of how
at least one Christian applied his faith in the context of the
Roman empire. The letter *1 Clement* is a culturally rather than
geographically Roman document, and from this observation
flows a further methodological question: How are we to
determine what might be thought to shape this document? Here,
in terms of methodology, the comparison with Paul's letter to the
Romans is striking. Is it the circumstances and theology of
the sender that shape his letter, or is it Clement's knowledge of
the situation in the Roman colony of Corinth, or is it some
combination of the two? Yet whereas Paul does seem to know
individuals and specific details about the situation in Rome
(Rom. 16), it is not clear that the same can be said of Clement's
knowledge of the situation in Corinth. If the author does not
know much of the situation in Corinth, then it is possible that his
portrayal of the apparent situation in Corinth is in fact indicative
of the situation in Rome.

That the letter was occasioned by news of trouble in Corinth
seems beyond doubt. This trouble is first introduced as an internal
dispute among the Corinthians that Clement characterises as an
'abominable and unholy sedition' (στάσις). It is caused by only a few
individuals, but has brought into disrepute the name of the whole
church (1.1). This sedition is referred to again at 3.3, where it is said
that on account of jealousy and envy, strife and sedition, those

without honour rose against those who were honoured. There then follows the main body of the letter, which is dedicated to an exhortation on the nature of the Christian life, a life that should be characterised by order and virtue. This emphasis on order is then applied to the church, and Clement writes that it is in contravention of the divine order established by God through the apostles and their successors that the Corinthians have deposed their elders (44.6). On account of only one or two individuals, and contrary to all that they have been taught in Christ, the established and ancient church of the Corinthians is in revolt (στασιάξειν) against the elders (47.6).

This picture of the situation in Corinth seems clear in so far as it goes, but it does seem striking and worthy of comment that it goes no further. Not only does Clement not argue specifically against those who have deposed the elders, save in so far that this transgresses the divine order, which he defends in general terms; he does not defend the deposed either, except in the most general of terms.

If the situation in Corinth cannot be shown to account for the detail of the arguments expressed in *1 Clement*, that detail might nevertheless be taken in one of two ways. On the one hand, it may be that much if not all of the detail is chosen because it is pertinent to the Corinthian situation in a way not apparent to us. Either formal constraints[51] or the assumption of shared knowledge may have led Clement not to put in writing details that would shed clear light on the situation at Corinth, but of which he was nevertheless aware. On such a reading, *1 Clement* is a text to use primarily in the search for Christianity at Corinth.[52]

On the other hand, it may be that Clement does in effect tell the Corinthians all that he knows. If so, then the argument he produces and the examples he adduces in his letter may reflect his own convictions as to how the Christian life should be lived corporately, and may reflect either his experience of or his vision for the life of the church in Rome rather than that in Corinth. On such a reading, *1 Clement* is a text to use primarily in the search for Christianity at Rome.

---

[51] L.L. Welborn, 'Clement, First Epistle of', *ABD*, vol. I, 1059.
[52] See, e.g., D.G. Horrell, *The Social Ethos of the Corinthian Correspondence*, 244–80.

Either way, all that we have to go on is a text from Rome, and there remains a significant gap between what we can say of that text and any reconstruction of the situation that may have lain behind it.

Adding further to this difficulty is that the writer increases the ambiguity with the suggestion that the position of the Roman church and that of Corinth is fundamentally the same. For, having outlined the dangers of jealousy, and having introduced the need for repentance as the beginning and basis of a truly Christian and orderly way of life, the letter continues, 'We are not only writing these things to you, beloved, for your admonition, but also to remind ourselves; for we are in the same arena, and the same struggle is before us' (7.1).

For Clement, what faces Roman and Corinthian alike is similar, and everything concerning which he writes could be equally familiar to Christians in either city, or indeed elsewhere in the Roman Mediterranean.

Remapping Trajectories: The *Shepherd of Hermas* as in and from but not (just) for Rome

Often confusing, possibly confused, one thing that cannot be denied to the *Shepherd of Hermas* is creativity. As Brown observes, the *Shepherd* is a 'long and puzzling work of Christian prophecy, sometimes evaluated as idiosyncratic mediocrity, other times as profound theology'.[53] Irenaeus spoke of it as Scripture,[54] Origen calls it divinely inspired,[55] and Eusebius reports that it was read publicly in churches.[56] These references, together with the suggestion that someone called Clement would send it abroad, may suggest that Hermas's revelations had some sort of official church status in Rome; certainly they point to its ongoing popularity.

The *Shepherd* may be placed firmly in Rome: it contains Roman imagery associated with the city, such as Hermas's use in one of his Similitudes of the image of the characteristically Italian agricultural practice of supporting vines on elm trees (Sim. 2.1–4), a technique

[53] Brown, 'Antioch and Rome', 203.
[54] Irenaeus, *Adversus Haereses* 4.20.2.
[55] Origen, *Commentarii in Romanos* 16.14.
[56] Eusebius, *Historia ecclesiastica* 3.3.6.

of planting known as the *arbustum*,[57] together with Roman but not 'Rome specific' references to Arcadia (Sim. 9.1.4) and to the Sibyl (Vis. 2.4.1). Yet it is not clear that it tells us much about Christianity at Rome that might be considered specific to that city. One key theme that does emerge is a clear concern for the relationship between rich and poor, a theme that has been given its clearest exposition by Carolyn Osiek.[58] Styling her monograph as 'a contribution to the social history of early Christianity'[59] Osiek aims not only to analyse the *Shepherd of Hermas* as a text, but also to interpret its function within its historical and social context, that is, Rome in the early to mid–second century. Addressing the question of 'the actual social situation of Hermas' community',[60] Osiek argues that Hermas's overriding concern is to call rich Christians to repentance for the way in which their wealth and business affairs have caused them to neglect the poor among them.[61] Direct address is always to the wealthy, never to the poor,[62] but Hermas is concerned to show that the poor can contribute something to the rich.[63] The one completes what is lacking in the other, and 'both together accomplish the work of the Lord'.[64]

In terms of social history, then, Osiek points to at least a part of the church in Rome where economic factors appear to be a pressing and practical concern. But, important though this is as a way of rooting the life of these early Christians in their sociological setting, the

---

[57] On which see C. Osiek, *Rich and Poor in the Shepherd of Hermas*, 78–83, 146–53. J.J. Paterson, 'Wine (Greek and Roman)', 1622, notes not only that the Roman expansion of viticulture was closely associated with the dissemination of classical culture, but also that the practice of growing vines up trees was 'such a distinctive feature of some of the most prized vineyards of Roman Italy ... that Pliny ... could claim that "classic wines can only be produced from grapes grown on trees"'.

[58] Osiek, *Rich and Poor.*

[59] Ibid. 3.

[60] Ibid. 14.

[61] Ibid. 39.

[62] Ibid. 55.

[63] With Sim. 2.6, where rich and poor contribute to each other; cf. *1 Clement* 38.2, where the rich contribute to the poor, but the poor offer nothing directly to the rich. See Osiek, *Rich and Poor*, 79–83.

[64] Ibid. 78ff.

question remains as to how if at all this problem was distinctive to or characteristic of Rome. That it was an issue in Rome is not in doubt, but we know that economic issues were of concern to Christians elsewhere also. Both James and the writings of Luke make much of the poor, and in so doing build on a long tradition in the Jewish Scriptures. Economic issues were prominent in the early Jerusalem church as recorded in Acts, and they appear to have raised their head in the practice of the Lord's Supper in Corinth. It is the symbolic economic interdependence between Gentile and Jew that Paul sees as vital to the collection for Jerusalem, which he introduces to the Romans as an example of how material blessings may be exchanged for spiritual ones (Rom. 15:26–7). The similarity with Hermas is striking, but this very similarity seems to point to a similarity of practice and belief among Christians across the empire rather than to anything distinctive to Rome.

Once again, a document located firmly at Rome may be illuminated just as well by what we know of Christianity from elsewhere in the Roman world as from Rome itself. This is not to deny the usefulness of Osiek's sociological reconstruction of the situation addressed by Hermas. It is merely to say that the address, though directed to at least some Christians in Rome in the first instance, might equally well be applied to Christians elsewhere, a reality recognised by the Christians in Rome having given to Clement a duty to copy their writings to others.[65]

Just as the writer of *1 Clement* was keen to establish the point that Christians in Corinth were in the same arena as Christians in Rome, so too a similar concern seems explicit in the instruction to Hermas that the content of his vision is to be transmitted to Christians beyond Rome as well as to those in Rome. For Hermas is instructed to make two copies of the book. One he will give to someone called Grapte who will exhort the widows and orphans, presumably in Rome. The other he will give to a certain Clement, who will send it

---

[65] Ibid. 11, suggests that the reference to Clement's duty is too obvious to be authentic, and that therefore it is a literary conceit designed to suggest that the *Shepherd* was written in the time of Clement and therefore to make it seem older than it was. This seems unlikely, however. If the author wanted the work read to his contemporaries, he could not have deceived them as to whether Clement was alive.

to the cities abroad, εἰς τὰς ἔᾳω πόλεις, for that is his duty (Vis. 2.4.3) Hermas's concern therefore, while primarily for Christians in Rome, is not limited to them. Nor, it would appear, should it ever be limited to an earthly city, for such a city can only ever be a temporary abode for those whose true city is far from the one in which they live (Sim. 1). Parallels with the Apocalypse, the origin of which is located usually in Roman Asia, spring to mind at once. Not only does that text reflect the belief that revelations specific to particular cities may be of interest to Christians elsewhere, but so too their own cities are of less importance than the new Jerusalem yet to come.

Parallel also to the Apocalypse is the Jewish feel of this Roman text. Angels abound, and the schema of two angels and two spirits, together with frequent exhortations against double-mindedness, might be taken to develop the two ways-type thinking found in Deuteronomy and Jeremiah and picked up also in *Barnabas* and the *Didache*. Leviathan appears in one vision (Vis. 4.1–2), but while scriptural themes and images abound, there is no explicit citation of Scripture.

Unlike *1 Clement* therefore Hermas does not base his authority on texts but on visions, and the only explicit appeal to a text treated as Scripture is a reference to the *Book of Eldad and Modat* (Vis. 2.3.4). Hermas's authority rests not on scriptural exegesis but on the revelation he is given. Thus although on some subjects, such as the role of the church as the continuation of Israel, *1 Clement* and the *Shepherd* present similar conclusions, they do so on different sources of authority. The leaders of the church are portrayed in *1 Clement* in terms of an ordered Levitical structure, albeit expressed in terms of order congenial to a Roman audience, but the *Shepherd* sees the Jewish prophets as the foundation on which the prophets of the Son of God are set (Sim. 9.15.4).

Nowhere is Hermas himself styled a prophet, but his own activity seems to be characteristic of what is generally understood of early Christian prophecy. The exhortation constantly made to Hermas both to lead and to proclaim the need for a morally upright and single-minded life is entirely consistent with the ethical grounds on which false and true prophets may be distinguished, as set out in Mandate 11.

This means therefore that any trajectory that sees the *Shepherd* as later than *1 Clement* and the latter as indicating the end of the authority of charismatic figures in the church is likely to struggle with the apparent co-operation between charismatic and institutional authority that is indicated in the *Shepherd*. No mention is made of prophetic activity in *1 Clement*, but the *Shepherd* depicts the prophet working with the elders. Hermas is probably not an elder (Vis. 3.1.7–9) although it is elders who preside over the church, to whom Hermas is to give the little book in which he records his vision and with whom he is to read it in Rome. Not only will Hermas read the book of his vision with the elders who are in charge of the church, but so too even the content of the revelations to Hermas is concerned with the need to distinguish between true and false prophecy. Thus the *Shepherd* and *1 Clement* might point to variety within the church at Rome, and could be representative of the outlooks of different house churches. It is possible that the elders in *Hermas* each lead a local house church and come together occasionally, or that Hermas addresses only one house church (whether or not there were others in Rome) over which a number of elders preside. Certainly *1 Clement* claims to represent the church at Rome, although whether all Roman Christians would have accepted this is unknown. We simply do not know, for we do not know how or whether to relate these texts to each other. They could be read as contemporary texts arising from within the umbrella of one dispersed Christian community, or either might pre-date the other.

If earlier evidence is to be drawn on, Romans 16 does seem to indicate a number of house churches, even if they were part of one church. References to the importance of hospitality point to the continuing significance of the house church in Rome, beginning with Paul's exhortation in Romans 12:13 to practise hospitality, continuing with references in *1 Clement*[66] and the *Shepherd*,[67] and

---

[66] 1.2 of the Corinthians; 10.7 of Abraham; 11.1 of Lot; 12.1, 3 of Rahab; 35.5 of the need to cast away inhospitality.

[67] Mandate 8.10, 'be hospitable, for in hospitality may be found the practice of good'; Sim. 9.27.2, where bishops and hospitable men may be synonymous: 'bishops and hospitable men who at all times received the servants of God into their houses gladly and without hypocrisy; and the bishops ever ceaselessly sheltered the destitute and the widows by their ministration, and ever behaved with holiness'; note also the note of Snyder, *Shepherd*, 153: 'Philoxenia was a mark of the leader from the beginning of the church …'

finally finding expression in the accounts of Justin's martyrdom at Rome.[68]

Yet even if there was but one church in Rome at the time of Paul, it is not clear that this situation necessarily continued to the period of *1 Clement* and the *Shepherd* and beyond. It is possible that rivalry among churches may have been one factor in the apparent tardiness of Rome to move towards a monarchical bishop. If in the mid-second century there were rival house churches in Rome focused on teachers as diverse as Justin, Marcion, Tatian, Valentinus and others, then it is possible that unity between different house churches was at least strained from an early date; certainly the author of *1 Clement* notes the presence of discord in Corinth, and it may be that in so doing he reflects unease about similar problems in Rome. Once again we cannot determine whether the two chief literary sources for Christianity at Rome represent the views of contemporaries in the same, in harmoniously coexisting, or even in rival house churches. Alternatively, they may well reflect different stages of Christianity in Rome. We know only their texts.

Conclusion

Three firm conclusions may be drawn from these texts, and it is with these conclusions as foundations that further hypothetical reconstruction should be built. The first is that in an instance such as this, *where texts may be located securely in space but not in time, it is necessary to study each in its own right and not to move with undue haste to draw trajectories between them.*

The second conclusion is that *such social and theological situations as can be discerned behind such texts need not be distinctive to their geographic settings, even if they are grounded in them*: similar situations might equally be found elsewhere under similar circumstances – such as any urban population made up of both free people and slaves, in which is found a significant Jewish element. From this comes the positive conclusion that a knowledge of differences

---

[68] Most conveniently in H. Musurillo (ed.), *The Acts of the Christian Martyrs*, 42–61.

between rich and poor in Rome derived from Hermas may be compared profitably if tentatively with similar discussions in other early Christian writings, even if such writings are not themselves thought to have originated in Rome. This thematic approach, which takes its evidence from literary sources, will not build up an archaeological profile of any one site, but may help us to understand elements of early Christianity that, although discussed broadly and generally, are nevertheless of value.

The third conclusion is that *this less city-specific approach has as its greatest merit that it follows the apparent approach of early Christians as seen in their writings, rather than the interests of modern scholars.* Thus this approach may be said to follow the cue of *1 Clement* in that he sees the Corinthian Christians as being in the same arena as those Roman Christians on whose behalf he writes, and the cue of the *Shepherd of Hermas*, which will be read outside as well as within the city of Rome.

On one level this challenge to recently proposed trajectories has led to what might be considered a negative approach to the investigation of early Christianity at Rome. For on the basis of two texts whose origin in Rome is indisputable I have argued that we know little of Christianity at Rome that is distinctive to that city and that might not be paralleled elsewhere in the Roman empire. But this is in fact a positive approach. Not only does it focus on the evidence of the texts themselves, rather than on hypothetical trajectories between them; but so too, in arguing for a picture of early Christianity as a movement whose theology did not permit itself to become overly localised, it suggests a degree of common belief and practice across centres of early Christianity that may have been neglected in the current scholarly emphasis on diversity in pre-Irenaean Christianity.

Bibliography

Aune, D.E., *Revelation 1–5* (WBC 52a; Dallas: Word Books, 1997)
Bowe, B.E., *A Church in Crisis: Ecclesiology and Paraenesis in Clement of Rome* (HDR 23; Minneapolis: Fortress Press, 1988)
Brown, R.E., and J.P. Meier (eds.), *Antioch and Rome: New Testament Cradles of Catholic Christianity* (London: Chapman, 1983)

Caragounis, C.C., 'From Obscurity to Prominence: The Development of the Roman Church between Romans and 1 Clement', K.P. Donfried and P. Richardson (eds.), *Judaism and Christianity in First-Century Rome* (Grand Rapids: Eerdmans, 1998)

Donfried, K.P., and P. Richardson (eds.), *Judaism and Christianity in First-century Rome* (Grand Rapids: Eerdmans, 1998)

Ferguson, E., 'Canon Muratori: Date and Provenance', *StPatr* 18 (1982), 677–83

—, review of Hahneman, *JTS* 44 (1993), 691–7

Grant, R.M., *The Apostolic Fathers: A New Translation and Commentary*, vol. 2: *First and Second Clement* (New York: Thomas Nelson, 1965)

Griffin, M., 'Urbs Roma, Plebs and Princeps', L.C.A. Alexander (ed.), *Images of Empire* (Sheffield: JSOT Press, 1991)

Hagner, D.A., *The Use of the Old and New Testaments in Clement of Rome* (Leiden: E.J. Brill, 1973)

Hahneman, G.M., *The Muratorian Fragment and the Development of the Canon* (Oxford: Clarendon Press, 1992)

Herron, T.J., 'The Most Probable Date of the First Epistle of Clement to the Corinthians', *StPatr* 21 (1989), 106–21

Horrell, D.G., *The Social Ethos of the Corinthian Correspondence* (Edinburgh: T. & T. Clark, 1996)

Jeffers, J.S., *Conflict at Rome: Social Order and Hierarchy in Early Christianity* (Minneapolis: Fortress Press, 1991)

Jefford, C.N., K.J. Harder and L.D. Amezaga, *Reading the Apostolic Fathers: An Introduction* (Peabody, MA: Hendrickson, 1996)

Lake, K., *Apostolic Fathers*, vol. 1 (Loeb; London: Heinemann, 1912)

Lane, W.L., 'Social Perspectives on Roman Christianity during the Formative Years from Nero to Nerva: Romans, Hebrews, 1 Clement', K.P. Donfried and P. Richardson (eds.), *Judaism and Christianity in First-Century Rome* (Grand Rapids: Eerdmans, 1998)

Maier, H.O., *The Social Setting of the Ministry as Reflected in the Writings of Hermas, Clement and Ignatius* (Waterloo, ON: Wilfrid Laurier University Press, 1991)

Musurillo, H. (ed.), *The Acts of the Christian Martyrs* (Oxford: Clarendon Press, 1972)

Osiek, C., *Rich and Poor in the Shepherd of Hermas: An Exegetical-Social Investigation* (CBQMS 15; Washington, D.C.: Catholic Biblical Association of America, 1983)

—, *Shepherd of Hermas: A Commentary* (Hermeneia; Minneapolis: Fortress Press, 1999)

Paterson, J.J., 'Wine (Greek and Roman)', in *The Oxford Classical Dictionary*, ed. S. Hornblower and A. Spawforth (Oxford: Oxford University Press, 1996³), 1622

Robinson, J.M., and H. Koester (eds.), *Trajectories Through Early Christianity* (Minneapolis: Fortress Press, 1971)

Snyder, G.F., *The Apostolic Fathers: A New Translation and Commentary*, vol. 6: *The Shepherd of Hermas* (New York: Thomas Nelson, 1968)

Streeter, B.H., *The Primitive Church: Studied with Special Reference to the Origins of the Christian Ministry* (London: Macmillan, 1929)

Tugwell, S., *The Apostolic Fathers* (Outstanding Christian Thinkers; London: Geoffrey Chapman, 1989)

Welborn, L.L., 'Clement, First Epistle of', *ABD* I, 1055–60

—, 'On the Date of First Clement', *BR* 24 (1984), 34–54

Wengst, K., *Pax Romana and the Peace of Jesus Christ*, trans. J. Bowden (Philadelphia: Fortress Press, 1987)

Wilson, J.C., *Towards a Reassessment of the Shepherd of Hermas: Its Date and Its Pneumatology* (Lewiston, NY: Edwin Mellen Press, 1993)